RESTORING PROPHETIC INTEGRITY

Scheherazade Daniels

Jeremiah One Nine Publishing

Columbus

Amplified Bible, http://www.lockman.org/tlf/copyright.php
"Scripture quotations taken from the Amplified® Bible, Scripture quotations marked (AMP) are taken from The Amplified Bible. Copyright © 1954, 1958, 1962, 1964, 1965, 1987 by The Lockman Foundation. Used by permission." (www.Lockman.org)

King James and New King James Version, Thomas Nelson http://www.thomasnelson.com/consumer/dept.asp?dept_id=11 17931&TopLevel_id=100000#RightsLicensing

1. Scripture quotations marked (KJV) are taken from the King James Version®. Copyright © 1982 by Thomas Nelson, Inc. Used by permission. All rights reserved.
2. Scripture quotations marked (NKJV) are taken from the New King James Version ®. Copyright © 1982 by Thomas Nelson, Inc. Used by permission. All rights reserved.

Any copying or duplication of this material and or its contents is subject to fines and penalties. This instructional manual was formatted for taking notes. Do not use or reproduce without written permission.

Submit written requests to: Harvest International Embassy, Attn: Apostle Clyde Daniel, PO Box 96 96, Reynoldsburg, Ohio 43068.

Copyright © 2013 by Clyde and Scheherazade Daniels
All Rights Reserved.

Daniels, Scheherazade
Restoring Prophetic Integrity / Clyde and Scheherazade Daniels

ISBN 978-0-9828738-2-3
1. Prophets – Training. 2. Prophetic Anointing.
Jeremiah One Nine Publishing – Columbus, Ohio –
614-949-6188

DEDICATION

This book is dedicated to my husband, Clyde Daniels. Over the years you have not only been an encouragement to me in trans-forming this manual into a book, but you have challenged me to go into deeper realms of the prophetic dimension.

I am eternally grateful for your support during this endeavor, and I am pleased to go forward with your blessings.

ACKNOWLEDGMENT

Writing a book is much like a journey. You need a map, lots of energy and determination. And you also need people to help you along your journey. I am grateful to the following people who assisted me.

To my husband, Clyde Daniels, who has been my coach and my launching pad. Thank you for challenging me to always go deeper. I love you now and forever. We share the same heart for the prophetic dimension and desire to see it restored and released in the earth in its fullness. I couldn't have walked this journey without you.

To my loving children, Shaheedrah, Kayla, Bethany, and my grandson, Joah — I love you all dearly. Thanks for your constant support, love and understanding when I had to take time away from you to work on this book.

Thanks to Prophet Sandee Hemphill for her inspiration, prophetic wisdom, prophetic words and help in publishing this book. You sacrificed time and sleep to help me and I am forever grateful.

I am appreciative of 3JPMedia, headed by Elder Allan Jr (JR) and JaQualia Leonard, for the book cover design. They became my one stop shop and my on-demand media professionals. Your prophetic creativity is greatly respected and appreciated. I love you guys.

Special thanks to Apostle Tim & Theresa Early, Apostle Sherri Dawson and Pastors Elliot and Josette Cohen. Over the years, each of you has been instrumental in cultivating and releasing the prophetic dimension at different stages of my life.

Thanks to the Harvest International Embassy family for receiving the prophetic spirit and allowing it flow. I look forward to greater dimensions being opened up to us.

Finally, thanks to Ramani Jackson and Minister Nicole Dobbs who helped review, proof-read and edit this book. I am thankful for your time and effort.

CONTENTS

Foreword *by Apostle Clyde Daniels*   9

Introduction   13

Section 1 —   17

Prophetic Foundation Overview
What is Prophecy?
Recognizing the Voice of God
The Holy Spirit and the Prophetic
Five Dimensions of the Prophetic Realm

— • — • — • — • — • — • — • — • —

Section 2 —   51

Attributes of a Prophet
Attributes of A Prophet
Hearing and Hearkening to the Voice of God
Pray and Intercede
Dreams and Visions (The Seer Dimension)

— • — • — • — • — • — • — • — • —

Section 3 —   79

Restoring Prophetic Integrity
Prophetic Integrity
Character Keys to Accuracy and Fruit-Filled
   Prophetic Ministry
Prophetic Contaminants
Checks and Balances of Prophetic Ministry
Instability in the Prophetic Dimension
Restoring Prophetic Integrity Wisdom Keys

Section 4 — 123

Mandate, Mantle and Mission
*Mandate, Mantle and Mission
Old and New Testament Prophets
Functions of a Mantled Prophet
Diverse Types of Prophets*

— • — • — • — • — • — • — • — • —

Section 5 — 153

Final Thoughts 155

Biography 157

FOREWORD

As far back as I can recall, I have always believed that God speaks to people and those that He speaks to have the ability to share it with others. So for me personally, when the Lord began to speak to me about His purpose for my life, I didn't think that was out of the ordinary. In fact, I assumed everyone could hear His voice; especially those who were His sheep.

I discovered that even though we all have the innate ability to hear the voice of the Lord, not everyone can. This is because of sin. Not just one's personal sin, but because of the original sin of man. Over time, the sin of Adam in the Garden caused the voice of God to become faint to all of mankind. And for this reason, God began to raise up different individuals to speak on His behalf. Most of these people were known as Prophets.

For the most part, these "Prophets" functioned and served as God's mouthpiece to mankind and the world they lived in. Some of these Prophets spoke to kings, nations, families, people groups and Prophets. Other Prophets carried out specific assignments from God

Foreword

such as calling a nation to repentance, destroying false altars, declaring victory over an enemy, delivering a people out of slavery, giving specific instructions, rebuking sinful behavior or the foretelling of a coming Savior King.

One example of a specific assignment is the Prophet Jeremiah, as written in Jeremiah 1:9-10 (NKJV), *9 Then the LORD put forth His hand and touched my mouth, and the LORD said to me: "Behold, I have put My words in your mouth.10 See, I have this day set you over the nations and over the kingdoms, To root out and to pull down, To destroy and to throw down, To build and to plant."* **God still uses His Prophets the same way today!**

As exciting as this may sound, many reject the idea of God speaking to man, especially through Prophets. Some argue this idea because Prophets — along with Apostles — have faded away and are no longer needed. This false premise is based upon the fact that we have the canon of text known as the Bible. But this is far from the truth!

Foreword

This false premise has caused much confusion to the Body of Christ regarding apostles and Prophets, especially the role and function of the New Testament Prophet. Because of this, many who believe they are called to be a Prophet do not receive the proper nurturing, training and cultivation they need in the prophetic. When this happens, the maturation process for the prophetic office is prolonged and sometimes aborted. The Prophet-in-training spends much time fighting to be affirmed, confirmed, heard, received, and accepted as a Prophet. This causes more damage than good and can cause many to reject Prophets and prophecy all together. *This is the reason for this book!*

As her Apostle and Pastor, I have seen Prophet Scheherazade Daniels grow into a very accurate and mature Prophet of God. She desires to see the prophetic dimension fully manifested as mature New Testament Prophets take their place in the Kingdom of God and release God's voice in the earth. Moses told Joshua his servant, "Oh, that all the LORD's people were **Prophets** *and* that the LORD would put

Foreword

His Spirit upon them! (see Numbers 11:29 NKJV)" **Restoring Prophetic Integrity** is a tool from the Lord to make this a reality.

I have witnessed the countless hours of preparation, study, prayer and consecration Prophet Scheherazade spent before the Lord to receive the revelation contained in this book. I have also witnessed years of implementing each of these principles in her life and ministry. In addition, Prophet Scheherazade has instilled them into the lives of other "Prophets" whom she has helped develop. She has served as a mentor, spiritual mother, friend, and as a visiting minister. Because of this, I am honored to write the foreword to **Restoring Prophetic Integrity** and recommend it to every person who is interested in learning more about the Office of the Prophet, and how they can function as an essential part of the Lord's government of the New Testament Church.

    Apostle Clyde Daniels —
    Senior Pastor
    Harvest International Embassy

INTRODUCTION

Restoring Prophetic Integrity was developed to give practical instruction for Prophets and Prophetic Ministers in operating in the prophetic dimension, so that the integrity of the prophetic dimension can be restored. Revelations 2:29 says, "He who has an ear, let him hear what the Spirit says to the Churches."

Within the Body of Christ there exists a profound need for a clear understanding regarding the Office of the Prophet. In addition, instruction and the proper acknowledgment of the Office are needed.

There has been a strong emphasis on personal prophecy in the Body of Christ. By this, the prophetic dimension has been limited to prophesying on one level—houses, cars, wives, and husbands. However, the prophetic dimension is so much more than personal prophecy.

The true essence of the prophetic dimension releases God's will in the earth, shifts atmospheres, turns hearts to God, and turns hearts back to God, just to name a few.

Introduction

This book will take the Believer through a fundamental review of the prophetic, through the nature and development of a Prophet, and bring about true understanding of the prophetic dimension. This will cause Prophets to know the true purpose of the prophetic and to know God's original desire and design for the prophetic dimension.

Restoring Prophetic Integrity is designed specifically for those members of the Body of Christ called by God to the Office of a Prophet. Its chief purpose is to bring clarity and understanding to the Body of Christ regarding the five-fold ascension gifts of the Office. Individuals will gain clear instructions for operating in the Office of Prophet.

Ephesians 4:11 tells us the five-fold ministry gift of the Prophet is not limited to preaching the gospel. It is also given to equip the Saints for the work of the ministry.

This development is accomplished through several means such as 1) Pointing the church in the direction

Introduction

God is speaking. 2) Training the saints for the work of the ministry. 3) Using prophesy to turn the hearts of the sons to the Father and the heart of the Father to the son.

Restoring Prophetic Integrity is not intended for the confirmation, commissioning or ordination of anyone to the five-fold governmental Office of the Prophet.

Section 1

Prophetic Foundation Overview

What is Prophecy?

ANY NUMBER OF DEFINITIONS COULD ANSWER THIS QUESTION. Our first definition is taken from Revelation 19:10. It tells us that "the testimony of Jesus is the Spirit of Prophecy." This means that prophecy is the vehicle of revelation that flows from Jesus Christ, therefore all prophecy must align itself with the Word of God. It must speak forth God's heart to the hearers regarding any situation that reveals Jesus as Christ.

The word "Christ" is translated from the Greek word *Christos*, which means the "Messiah King." Therefore, prophecy should exalt the King, the Kingship of Christ and the eternal purpose of the Kingdom of God.

In its simplest form, prophecy is speaking forth the heart, mind, will, purposes, plans, and council of God. Prophecy is brought forth under the inspiration of the Holy Spirit. Prophets must have a clear understanding of prophecy and its various operations.

RESTORING PROPHETIC INTEGRITY

Most people ask "How do I know God is speaking to me?" This is a valid question. It can be explained by understanding the different voices that speak to us on a daily basis.

In John 10:27, Jesus states, "My sheep hear My voice, and I know them, and they follow me." The most effective way to know the voice of God is to spend time praying and mediating on scripture. According to scripture, this is the biblical format. Luke 18:1 says that men always ought to pray and not lose heart. 1 Thessalonians 5:17 says we are to pray without ceasing. Moreover, in Psalm 119:148, David indicates that his eyes are awake through the night watches that he may mediate on God's word. Biblical meditation is focusing one's mind on scripture. As one prays and meditates, recognizing the voice of God becomes easier.

Recognizing the voice of God is imperative to releasing accurate prophetic utterances and moving in the prophetic dimension. This is important because releasing any other voice while ministering prophetically would lead to error.

The Four Voices That Speak to Us

As believers, it is our responsibility to recognize how and when God is speaking to us. We must fine-tune our hearing to recognize His voice at all times. There are four voices that routinely speak to us. They are:
1) The Voice of God or the Spirit of God
2) Voice of our Emotions or Conscience
3) Voice of Demonic Influence
4) Voice of Outside Human Influences

We must differentiate His voice from all other voices. It is God's desire that His voice becomes louder and clearer than any other voice we hear. Therefore, learning to distinguish God's voice and respond accordingly is a must.

1. **The Voice of God or the Spirit of God** – The voice of God speaks through our spirit or heart. When Samuel was learning God's voice, God was speaking through to his spirit. God's voice resounded in his spirit so loud that in the natural realm he thought Eli was calling him.

2. **Voice of our Emotions or Conscience** – This voice is also called the voice of self or the voice of flesh. This voice seeks self-gratification based upon selfish wants. Ananias and Sapphira are an example. In Acts 5:1-11, we see that Ananias and Sapphira sold a possession and kept back part of the proceeds for selfish reasons. The Voice of Emotions can speak and influence your fleshly desires.

3. **Voice of Demonic Influence** – This voice generally intrudes the mind and influences our thoughts, producing unfruitful behavior. In Genesis 3, the serpent influenced Eve's thoughts and deceived her into thinking she was not going to die if she ate from the forbidden tree.

4. **Voice of Outside Human Influences** – This voice is also known as the voice of humanism and speaks to influence your behavior or shift you out of the will of God. In the story of Sampson and Delilah (Judges 16), Delilah pestered Sampson and insisted he tell her where his strength laid. Due to the vexing of his soul, he revealed the secret to his strength. He

RESTORING PROPHETIC INTEGRITY

did not realize the Lord had left him. The voice of human influence can vex the soul and cause you to make wrong decisions. You become desensitized to the Spirit of God.

Our human nature has the tendency to gravitate to the voice that brings the most self-gratification and pleasure. The voice of emotions (flesh), the voice of demonic influence, and the voice of human influence are at constant conflict with the voice of God. Each voice has its own agenda that hinders the voice of God from being heard and understood.

Here are examples of these ungodly spirits:
— The voice of **demonic influence** wants to control God's people and prevent them from ever discovering God's plan for their lives, both individually and corporately.
— The **voice of emotions** (flesh) will seek self-gratification and only seeks what's in it for them. It is rooted in selfishness and looks for its own blessing. It keeps others from entering the place where the Lord's

blessing is commanded — that place of unity (Psalm 133:3).

— The **voice of humanism** seeks to remove Christ and all things pertaining to God, the Church, Christianity and the Kingdom of God from the earth in order to establish an "anti-Christ" culture. This would create a Godless society where the highest authority would be man's authority which is finite in understanding (see Proverbs 14:12, 1 Corinthians 1:20-25, 1 Corinthians 3:18-21, James 3:13-18, and Psalm 111:10). Submitting to either of these voices brings you into direct opposition to God's will for you. Study these scriptures to gain further insight:

> Roman 8:7 - *"[That is] because the mind of the flesh [with its carnal thoughts and purposes] is hostile to God, for it does not submit itself to God's Law; indeed it cannot." (Amplified)*

> Galatians 5:16-18 *"But I say, walk and live [habitually] in the [Holy] Spirit [responsive to and controlled and guided by the Spirit]; then you will certainly not gratify the cravings and desires of the flesh (of human nature without*

RESTORING PROPHETIC INTEGRITY

God). For the desires of the flesh are opposed to the [Holy] Spirit, and the [desires of the] Spirit are opposed to the flesh (godless human nature); for these are antagonistic to each other [continually withstanding and in conflict with each other], so that you are not free but are prevented from doing what you desire to do. But if you are guided (led) by the [Holy] Spirit, you are not subject to the Law (Amplified)."

1 Corinthians 10: 20-21 *"No, I am suggesting that what the pagans sacrifice they offer [in effect] to demons (to evil spiritual powers) and not to God [at all]. I do not want you to fellowship and be partners with diabolical spirits [by eating at their feasts]. You cannot drink the Lord's cup and the demons' cup. You cannot partake of the Lord's table and the demons' table (Amplified)."*

REFLECTIVE QUESTIONS

1. In the simplest form, what is prophecy?

2. "The spirit of Prophecy is the testimony of Jesus." Where is this scripture found?

3. Complete this sentence: It is our (add content) to discover how God (add content) to us.

4. All prophetic revelation must (add content).

5. What is the Greek word for Christ?

6. All prophetic revelation must (add content).

7. What is the agenda of the voice of demonic influence?

8. What are the primary ways God speaks to you?

9. What are the four voices that speak to mankind?

10. What is God's desire regarding His voice?

The Holy Spirit and the Prophetic

The Holy Spirit

Who is the Holy Spirit? The Holy Spirit is the third person of the Godhead that is resident in the earth. He is the presence of God in the earth. The Holy Spirit indwells believers as He fills them. This is the seal of our salvation. Because of these attributes, He is called the Comforter, the Helper, the Promise of the Father and the Spirit of Christ. Every New Testament Prophet of God has an up close and personal relationship with the Holy Spirit and is filled with Him. The Bible says there were Prophets in the Old Testament who were filled with the Spirit of God (Genesis 41:38; Exodus 31:3; Daniel 5:14).

The Holy Spirit has many attributes that He uses to empower believers to live a Spirit-filled life here on earth.

Attributes of the Holy Spirit

Attribute	Reference
He is the Teacher of all things	John 14:26
He guides us into all truths	John 16:13
He is the source of Dunamis power	Acts 1:8
He is a revealer of hearts	John 14:23
He convicts the world of sin and righteousness	John 16:8-10
He speaks what is to come	John 16:13
He gives revelation knowledge and understanding of things pertaining to God	1 Corinthians 2:10-16
He makes intercession for us	Romans 8:27
He searches the hearts of man	Romans 8:27
He is the seal of our salvation and the guarantee of the Believers inheritance	Ephesians 1:13-14
He is the consecrator to those called into ministry	Acts 13:2
He is a giver of the Gifts of the Spirit	1 Corinthians 12:12:4-11

RESTORING PROPHETIC INTEGRITY

The Gifts of the Holy

The Gifts of the Holy Spirit are given to the Body of Christ to equip them for service. Every Believer should have a functional understanding of the nine gifts of the Spirit and their relevance to the prophetic dimension. It is the Holy Spirit who reveals the prophetic word to the one who minister's prophetically. There is no separation of the prophetic dimension from the power and presence of the Holy Spirit (see 1 Corinthians 14).

In 1 Corinthians 12: 8-10, nine Gifts of the Holy Spirit are listed. These gifts can be separated into three categories: power gifts, vocal gifts and revelatory gifts. Because of the connection between the prophetic and the Holy Spirit, many times the gifts operate within the prophetic dimension.

We'll briefly explore the **Power Gifts:**

The Gift of Healing

The Gift of Healing is the supernatural ability to heal without human assistance. A healing occurs when the power of God causes the body's natural healing process to supersede time and a healing is suddenly manifested.

The woman with the issue of blood in Mark 5:25-29 is an example of the Gift of Healing. This gift works in conjunction with the Gift of Prophecy. There are times when the Gift of Healing includes human efforts that are led by the Holy Spirit.

The Gift of Healing is often used in areas where infirmity is lodged, or there is an attack on the human body. In Luke 13:11-13, Jesus healed a woman with the spirit of infirmity and she was made whole. God may also use human instrumentation and medical treatment in conjunction with this gift. For example, someone can have a spirit-filled medical professional that sees an infirmity and have the ability to pray and release supernatural healing to bring forth wholeness.

The Working of Miracles

The Working of Miracles is the supernatural power of God to intervene in a person's life without any human assistance. It generally manifests when all natural resources have been exhausted and no human effort can bring forth the desired resolution. The Working of Miracles is a display of God's power beyond the natural.

It operates closely with the gift of faith and healing to bring authority over demons, sickness, and spiritual wickedness of this age. See the example in John 2; Jesus performs his first miracle when he turns water into wine.

The Gift of Faith

The Gift of Faith is a supernatural endowment to totally trust in God without any doubt. It has the ability to combat unbelief and has the ability to meet difficult situations head on with absolute trust in God and His word. In Luke 7:6-10, the Centurion had so much faith that he sent a message to Jesus telling him that he did not need to come to his house, only send his word and his servant will be healed. Because of his faith, his servant was made whole. Jesus counted it to him as having great faith.

RESTORING PROPHETIC INTEGRITY

Here's a look at the **Revelatory Gifts:**

The Word of Knowledge

The Word of Knowledge is the supernatural revelation of God's divine will and plan for any situation. It is supernatural insight or understanding of circumstances that are revealed by revelation. Although Jesus was the Word manifested, He prophesied to the woman at the well (John 4:5-28). A Word of Knowledge may also refer to knowledge of God or of the things that belong to God, as related in the gospel of the Kingdom.

The Word of Wisdom

The Word of Wisdom is God's perspective for accomplishing His will in a given situation. It has the Divine power to appropriate supernatural insight in problem solving. The word of wisdom is the mind of Christ to apply knowledge appropriately with discernment. As Jesus ministered, he spoke parables as words of wisdom.

RESTORING PROPHETIC INTEGRITY

The Discerning of Spirits

The Discerning of Spirits is the supernatural power to detect the spiritual realm and their activities. It has the ability to determine if they are of the Kingdom of God (Angels) or the kingdom of darkness (demons). It is not birthed out of suspicion but of a supernatural revelation from the Holy Spirit. Paul was operating in the discerning of spirits in Acts 16:16-19. When in operation, it has the ability to reveal the plans of the enemy and its forces.

Our last group is the **Vocal Gifts:**

Diversity of Tongues

Diversity of Tongues is the supernatural utterance in languages that are not known to the speaker. However, these languages must exist somewhere in the world today. They may be revived from past culture or be an "unknown tongue" (revelation) as a means of Holy Spirit inspired communication. The initial manifestation may serve as a sign and evidence of the indwelling of the Holy Spirit (baptism). Tongues function as an operation of the mind of the Spirit— not the human mind. Tongues may manifest with prophecy and the Gift of Interpretation of Tongues (Is. 28:11; Mark 16:17; Acts 2:4; 10:44-48; 19:1-7; 1 Cor. 12:10, 28-31; 13:1-3; 14:2, 4-22, 26-32).

Interpretation of Tongues

The Interpretation of Tongues is the supernatural power to reveal the meaning of unknown tongues. It is not a translation but a literal interpretation with exact meaning of the unknown tongue (1 Corinthians 14:27).

The Gift of Prophecy

We'll examine this gift in greater detail later. One key- note pertaining to prophecy is that some who have this gift are not prophets, yet they have a highly accurate manifestation of this gift. The Gift of Prophecy was activated in those who were filled – baptized with the Holy Spirit in the book of Acts 19:6.

RESTORING PROPHETIC INTEGRITY

The revelatory gifts of the Holy Spirit and the Gift of Prophecy are sometimes intertwined with each other. All three sets of gifts, the **Power Gifts**, **Revelatory Gifts** and **Vocal Gifts**, can and will flow together. This is especially seen in deliverance, healing and miracle services.

REFLECTIVE QUESTIONS

1. Why did God give us the Revelatory Gifts?

2. The Gifts of the Holy Spirit can be separated into three (3) categorizes. Circle your answer:
   A) Power   B) Sensory   C) Vocal
   D) Hearing   E) Revelatory

3. What gift has the ability to heal without human assistance?

4. The Working of Miracles is (add content).

5. Define the supernatural endowment used to totally trust God without any doubt.

6. Supernatural utterances in languages that are not known to the speaker are called what?

7. What constitutes the supernatural insight or understanding of situations that are revealed by the Holy Spirit?

8. What is the supernatural power that enables you to detect the spiritual realm and their activities?

REFLECTIVE QUESTIONS

9. What describes the mind of Christ with the ability to apply knowledge appropriately with discernment?

10. What gift has the power to reveal the meaning of an unknown utterance?

11. What do we call Holy Spirit-inspired and anointed words that we release?

12. Match the following —

    P = Power Gifts   **R** = Revelatory   **V** = Vocal

    ___ Gift of Faith

    ___ Discernment of Spirits

    ___ Gift of Prophecy

    ___ Gift of Healing

    ___ Word of Knowledge

    ___ Working of Miracles

    ___ Word of Wisdom

    ___ Diversity of Tongues

    ___ Interpretation of Tongues

Five Dimensions of the Prophetic

This overview covers the major aspects of prophetic demonstration and manifestation. Some features are unique to the realm discussed, while other overlap.

Spirit of Prophecy
The testimony of Jesus Christ is the spirit of prophecy. As mentioned before, the very nature or essence of prophecy is to give a pure witness of Jesus Christ. In the scripture referenced, the angel told John to worship God and then revealed that the testimony of Jesus Christ is the Spirit of prophecy. "And I fell at his feet to worship him. But he said to me, 'See that you do not do that! I am your fellow servant, and of your brethren who have the testimony of Jesus. Worship God! For the testimony of Jesus is the spirit of prophecy'" (Revelation 19:10 - NKJV). For this reason the spirit of prophecy is greatly released through worship.

When the Holy Spirit manifests His Shekinah Glory, there is a release of prophecy that anyone in the midst can be inspired to use to release a word of prophecy.

RESTORING PROPHETIC INTEGRITY

1 Corinthians 14:31 says "For you can all prophesy one by one, that all may learn and all may be encouraged."

Gift of Prophecy
The Gift of Prophecy is one of the nine gifts of the Holy Spirit outlined in 1 Corinthians 12:7-11. It's a manifestation of the Spirit of God that happens when someone receives the baptism of the Holy Spirit (see Acts 2:17-18, Acts 19:6; I Corinthians 12:1-10; 14:1-6). *Note: The Spirit of Prophecy and the Gift of Prophecy are for edification, exhortation and comfort. It is important to note that the Gift of Prophecy is different from the Office of a Prophet, and just because someone flows in prophecy doesn't make someone a Prophet.*

Office of a Prophet
The Prophet is the second ascension gift given when Jesus ascended. Prophets are not limited to only exhortation, edification and comfort. They can bring a word of rebuke, reproof, correction or direction in the Spirit of Love. The Prophet does not operate out of the Gift of Prophecy but out of a mantle given by the Lord Jesus Himself.

RESTORING PROPHETIC INTEGRITY

The Prophet releases the prophetic dimension of Christ in the earth. Their mantle has the ability to activate others to prophesy and release the Prophetic Dimension into a sphere of influence. The Prophet has the ability to give direction, whereas one with the prophetic gifting alone cannot always do this with accuracy (This is merely a snapshot of Ephesians 4:11 — not an in-depth look at the Office of the Prophet).

Prophetic Presbytery

Prophetic Presbytery is a team of Prophets or prophetic ministers. Typically, they are elders of a local assembly who are recognized as having prophetic authority. However, their sphere of authority is not limited to the local church. The prophetic presbytery is not formed from novices. They carry a responsibility to provide government within a local church, an organization or a region.

When a prophetic presbytery is in operation, they carry delegated authority to release and activate individuals into their purposes in God. They display a prophetic leadership anointing that is given to those who are prophetically mature (I Timothy 4:14, Acts 13:1-3 and 2 Timothy 1:6).

Prophecy of Scripture

There is no higher level of prophecy than prophecy of scripture. It is also the purest dimension of prophecy. All other dimensions MUST line up with the Holy Scriptures.

Prophecy of scripture is infallible; it is without mistake. Other prophetic dimensions may be infiltrated with the human element as well as a grace to prophesy in part (1 Corinthians 13:8-9; 2 Timothy 3:16, 2 Peter 1:20-21). To be scripturally valid, all prophecy and revelation must line up with the Word of God.

REFLECTIVE QUESTIONS

1. What are the five dimensions of Prophecy?

2. The Gift of Prophecy is for (3 responses needed).

3. Under what manifestation of the Spirit can anyone prophesy?

4. Which dimension of Prophecy does not operate out of the gift of prophecy alone but by a mantle?

5. The Spirit of Prophecy is greatly released through what?

6. What is the highest level of prophecy?

7. Prophecy gives what of Jesus Christ?

8. Tell what a Prophetic Presbytery is not.

9. What is prophecy of scripture?

10. Prophetic Presbytery is a (add answer) anointing given to the (add answer).

RESTORING PROPHETIC INTEGRITY

Types of Prophetic Operations

Scripture shows us the Lord's method of communicating to the Prophets was unique in the way each received revelation, and in how they were released in the earth. This is called **Prophetic Operations**.

Likewise, today's prophetic minister operates in a primary prophetic flow. However, there are times when a seasoned prophetic minister may find himself operating in more than one flow as the Lord desires to release His Word.

There will still be a primary way in which the prophetic flows through him. However, every flow has its place and no operation is greater than the other.

Scripture records several Hebrew and Greek words used for the word 'Prophet.' Additionally, the New Testament records several Greek words that define both 'prophecy' and 'to prophesy.' A brief compilation of these words is listed on the following page.

RESTORING PROPHETIC INTEGRITY

Propheteuo — 4395. *propheteuo* [prof-ate-yoo'-o] from 4396; to foretell events, divine, speak under inspiration, exercise the prophetic office: —prophesy.

Propheteia — 4394. *propheteia* [prof-ay-ti'-ah] from 4396 ("prophecy"); prediction (scriptural or other):— prophecy, prophesying.

Prophetikos — 4397. *prophetikos* [prof-ay-tik-os'] from 4396; pertaining to a foreteller ("prophetic"):--of prophecy, of the prophets.

Please see Acts 2:17; 1 Corinthians 14:1; 1 Timothy 4:14; 2 Peter 2:19.

The other words not only describe the different types of communication methods, but also reveal different methods in which one operates.

Flow Description: (HB) = Hebrew (GK) = Greek Online Hebrew and Greek Lexicon (www.eliyah.com/lexicon.html)

RESTORING PROPHETIC INTEGRITY

Nabi *(Hb) Nabi* — prophet – *nabiyah* – prophetess is the official word for Prophet – this one bubbles – John 7:38. In this type of prophetic flow the word bubbles up like an eruption. Generally, when the word comes forth the one who receives will release what they are hearing and as they speak the word keeps flowing. This flow is like the voice of many waters (Revelation 14:2). A cistern of the deep opens up and prophecy can flow continually.

Ro'eh *(Hb) Ro'eh* — 1 Sam 9:9 – seer or prophet – 7204 Ro'eh ro-ay' for 7203; prophet; Roeh, an Israelite:--Haroeh. Ro'eh is related to the word seer. One who sees visions. This type of flow is typically received by those who have visual learning styles. When receiving prophetic word, the receiver may see pictures, maps, images and open visual scenes. There also are those who experience vivid dreams communicating to the receiver a message from the Lord (Acts 2:17).

Chozeh or ***Chozen*** *(Hb) Chozeh or Chozen* — a beholder in a vision; seer - 2374 chozeh kho-zeh' active participle of 2372; a beholder in vision; also a compact (as looked upon with approval): — agreement, prophet, see that, seer, (star-gazer). A seer who is specifically a prophet (1 Chronicles 29:29). In scripture this prophetic type is mostly associated with the service of a king, i.e. Nathan to David. Today they also could be assigned to a king, president, prime minister, CEO, mayor, governor, Apostle or those who are in positions of authority. They have a type of prophetic grace to be personal intercessors and have authority and access to those to which they are assigned. If a Prophet who flows as a chosen vessel was assigned to the president, they will somehow have a grace to access those in authority directly or indirectly. *"A man's gift maketh room for him, and bringeth him before great men."* — Proverbs 18:16

Shamar *(Hb) Shamar* — 8104 shamar shaw-mar' a primitive root; properly, to hedge about (as with thorns), i.e. guard; generally, to protect, attend to, etc.:--beward, be circumspect, take heed (to self), keep(-er, self), mark, look narrowly, observe, preserve, regard, reserve, save (self), sure, (that lay)

RESTORING PROPHETIC INTEGRITY

wait (for), watch(-man). Jeremiah 51:12. Shamar is a type of watchman, meaning to guard, keeper of the people. This type of prophetic flow operates in different levels of spiritual warfare and willing to go into warfare on behalf of another.

Nataf *(Hb)* *Nataf* — 5197 nataph naw-taf' a primitive root; to ooze, i.e. distil gradually; by implication, to fall in drops; figuratively, to speak by inspiration:-- drop(-ping), prophesy(-et). Amos 7:16. To preach, drop as dew from Heaven, to speak by heavenly inspiration. This is a dimension of revelation that fall like dew to the receiver instantly. Usually prophetic counselors operate in this flow. Many who operate in this prophetic flow will often times appear to receive downloads from the Throne of God.

Prophetes *(Gk)* — 4396. prophetes prof-ay '-tace from a compound of 4253 and 5346; a foreteller ("prophet"); by analogy, an inspired speaker; by extension, a poet: prophet. Inspired messenger who speaks on behalf of God. Typically this is misinterpreted to say that all preachers are prophets because they speak the word of God, so there is no need for prophets in the New Testament church. Just remember that Agabus and certain inspired prophets gave guidance in the New Testament (Acts 11:28 and 21:10).

REFLECTIVE QUESTIONS

Please take the time required to reflect upon these two questions and answer them to your best knowledge.

What is your primary operation in the prophetic?

Why do you believe so?

Section 2

Attributes of a Prophet

Attributes of a Prophet

PROPHETS SHARE CERTAIN INHERENT CHARACTERISTICS. As stated previously, prophets are very unique, yet they all share the commonality of the call, the process and commissioning.

The process of prophetic maturity and the commissioning will be different for each prophet, based upon his mantle, mandate and mission, regardless of how the prophet is called. Their development is subject to the Lord's will. These attributes are visible — their commonality — in the actions of the Old Testament prophets.

Calling

No one can self-appoint themselves to the Office of a Prophet. The call must come from God. Deuteronomy 18:15 states, *"The LORD your God will raise up for you a Prophet like me from your midst, from your brethren. Him you shall hear."* Moreover, the Bible says to desire spiritual gifts — not a fivefold office.

RESTORING PROPHETIC INTEGRITY

The Office of Prophet is one of the ascension gifts that Jesus gave when He arose from the grave. However, HE calls select individuals for this task and anoints them in their calling. To clarify further, let's examine two of the most prominent Old Testament Prophets — Jeremiah and Samuel.

God told Jeremiah that he knew him when he was in his mother's womb, and ordained (called) him to be a Prophet to the nations (Jeremiah 1:5). Jeremiah did not want the call due to the heavy responsibility that it entailed. However, when God ordained him, Jeremiah received the divine seal of approval. He understood that his assignment was to go forth, and proclaim that which God was speaking to him. When God called Samuel, he spoke to him several times. Samuel thought it was Eli calling him (I Samuel 3:4-11). Bear in mind that God spoke audibly to both of them.

In like manner, most of today's Prophets have been called by God to the Office of Prophet by God's audible voice. Others have recognized their call because an Apostle or Prophet brought them clarity.

RESTORING PROPHETIC INTEGRITY

Some who thought they heard the call were blessed to receive the release and activation of other five-fold gifts.

P.I.T (Purifying Intense Testing) Process

The process of purification is the process in which God turns up the heat in your life. This process is designed to bring all the impurities to the surface so God can remove them. God designs a process of intense testing and trials specifically for you. In doing so He can work through you and in you to bring out that which is pure. In essence, when you are going through your testing and trials, God is purifying every aspect of your being.

Every person who has been called to the Office of a Prophet has endured some hard seasons of life. This is why most Prophets don't want to answer the call. The process is extremely difficult, but EXTREMELY necessary in order to produce the mouthpiece God desires. You cannot be used to speak on his behalf unless you can endure your purification process. Isaiah recognized the seriousness of the purification process.

RESTORING PROPHETIC INTEGRITY

In Isaiah 6, he indicated that the angels took the coals from the altar and cleansed his tongue. Purifying is a great challenge. Anything or anyone who is going to be pure must be purified by the fire of God.

The PIT process requires much prayer and crying out to God. There are times when there seems to be no rest from the warfare and trials that come. However, it is during this time that God is shaping you. God uses the PIT process to develop you into the Prophet He has called you to be. He is building you for the mandate He has given you.

Your process was designed just for you, so you will be able to carry the weight of the call. Quite often, during the PIT process, the Prophet begins to live the message that he carries. The title of Prophet or Prophetess may sound good; however, one must experience and understand the PIT process. More than likely it makes you want to back up and try to avoid the call at all costs.

RESTORING PROPHETIC INTEGRITY

Most Prophets have attempted to avert the PIT process. Look at Jeremiah; he gave excuses, saying, "but I am a child." Isaiah did something similar. He said, "but I am a man of unclean lips." Most Prophets understand that the price for the anointing is costly. They also understand that the prophetic anointing will cost them everything that they are, and everything they have, to walk in it.

The purpose of purifying and pressing during the PIT process is to bring forth purity of the following areas:

Spiritual Circumcision — The Gilgal experience is painful but necessary. Once a Prophet is called, one of the first things the Lord will do is spiritually circumcise you. Circumcision rolls the reproach of Egypt off of you and creates a new wineskin. Egypt represents the mindset, ideals, ideology, customs and cultures we have previously identified ourselves with. Egypt must be removed so we can correctly align ourselves with His kingdom purposes for our lives. This is not an easy adjustment for a Prophet because it cuts away a lot of extra things. It's the removal of things that are not necessary or things that will hinder the Lord's will.

Character Testing — God tests everything about your character. This testing reveals the flaws and traits that you have come to live with and release over the course of your life. More than likely, these were not Godly character traits, rather ungodly traits which were developed out of our old nature — prior to salvation. During the PIT process, it is necessary to let Christ develop your Godly character in private so that when it is time for public ministry, your character can stand under the weight of the assignment.

The Creative Force of the Tongue — As a Prophet, your tongue will either carry a blessing or a curse; it will not carry both. Due to the creative nature of the Prophet, you will have to watch what and how you say things

RESTORING PROPHETIC INTEGRITY

because it will be created in the spirit realm. This is why James said blessing and cursing should not come out of the same mouth (James 3:10). As you are casually speaking, remember to watch what you say. Idle conversations cannot produce the fruit of the spirit.

Motives — Motives are critical to the lifeblood of a Prophet. This area will ALWAYS be tested; you must constantly check your motives. Some examples of wrong motives are:
1) Desiring to be a Prophet for status and respect, 2) Looking for personal benefits such as an armor bearer, 3) Having control and domination over others.

Others desire to be a Prophet for monetary gain. These impure and selfish motives have contributed to the hindrance of accepting the gift (1 Corinthians 13:1-8).

RESTORING PROPHETIC INTEGRITY

Integrity — This is another major area of testing. It is important that Prophets make sure that when testing occurs, they continue to walk in integrity and love. Do NOT let your good be evil spoken of.

Building Faith — During this process your faith will be tested. You must know that God has called you and that your faith in Him will withstand any test.

Confidence in Knowing God's Voice — The process of purification causes you to hear the voice of God more clearly. It is also during this time that you gain confidence to know and discern between the voice of the enemy and the voice of human influence that is often in conflict with the voice of God and the voice of your emotions.

Obedience and Submission — Submission is a "bad" word to some Prophets; they don't want to hear it.

RESTORING PROPHETIC INTEGRITY

Moreover, our entire relationship with Jesus Christ is based upon obedience and submission. God tests your obedience to see if you will follow him and no other. Visit the story of the old Prophet and the young Prophet (1 Kings 13). God established our covenant with Him through submission. We must totally submit to God and rely on Him in order to fulfill His will for our lives.

Suffering from Rejection (their entire life) — This is when the 'woe is me' syndrome kicks in. This was Elijah's cry after his Mt. Carmel show-down. "I am the only one left who wants God. Nobody likes me and nobody understands me," (I Kings 19:10).

Commissioning

The act of commissioning is the sending forth in power. When your gift has been proven and you have become seasoned, the Lord then commissions you and unveils you to the Body of Christ. Such were the examples of Elijah, Elisha, Paul and Timothy, and also the disciples who were sent forth to demonstrate the Kingdom of God. As a Prophet, you must wait on the Lord for His timing of commissioning and being sent forth. There have been Prophets who "went," but were not "sent." Jeremiah 23:21 tells us, *"I have not sent these prophets, yet they ran, I have not spoken to them, yet they prophesied"* — NKJV.

In addition to the call, the process and commissioning, there are other characteristics of the Prophet which should be evident in their lives. The characteristics will more than likely be developed before being commissioned for ministry to the body.

Hears and Hearkens to the Voice of God

Another attribute of a Prophet is the ability to hear the voice of God, hearken to Him and move in obedience. As Prophets, we must listen with spirit ears and see with spirit eyes. We must move forth in faith and obedience to God. It is imperative that a Prophet hearkens and moves swiftly when he receives a message from the Lord.

RESTORING PROPHETIC INTEGRITY

Pray and Intercede

The subject of prayer and intercession is a broad topic, yet it is very simple as it relates to the Prophet and the prophetic dimension. In the prophetic dimension, prayer is the vehicle used to receive prophetic words, messages, dreams, visions, and for our spiritual encounters with the Lord.

Although they are different in the prophetic and the prophetic dimension, they work hand in hand when it comes to relating, receiving, and releasing communication from the Lord.

Prayer and intercession are demonstrated through-out scripture. In innumerable instances, the Lord spoke to his servants through prayer. The same holds true for us today.

As the prophetic minister understands and develops his prophetic gifting, they activate an elevated level of the prayer and intercessory anointing. This anointing allows them to pray and receive communication from the Lord.

There are three areas of prayer and intercession that are activated when a person starts to develop their prophetic gifting:

1) Increased Spiritual Discernment

Prophets and Intercessors have discernment and insight into spiritual realms. In the process of prayer and intercession, discernment is increased and their spiritual senses become extremely keen to spiritual atmospheres, and sensitive to the voice of God (Hebrews 5:14).

2) Increase of Grace for Prayer and Fasting

Most prophetic ministers have come to understand and develop a lifestyle of prayer and fasting. They see prayer and fasting as an important key to receiving prophetic words from the Lord. The Lord will give the

RESTORING PROPHETIC INTEGRITY

prophetic minister a special grace to fast and pray because they are being developed as mouthpieces of the Lord.

Prayer—along with fasting—helps to maintain prophetic accuracy and integrity. Continuous prayer creates open dialogue with the Holy Spirit. Fasting keeps the flesh under control and under the subjection to the spirit man.

3) Increase in Prayer Assignments

Prophets and prophetic ministers should pray constantly for people and their situations. Luke 18:1 says that men ought to always pray. Prophets feel the heartbeat of God and pray according to what grieves the Lord. It is during these times that compassion is birthed in a Prophet and they learn how to prophesy out of a loving spirit. The type of prophetic words and messages that will be received will call for the Prophet or prophetic minister to pray regarding the word.

RESTORING PROPHETIC INTEGRITY

We are admonished by 1 Thessalonians 5:17 to pray without ceasing. There are times when God will give a prophetic word that He doesn't allow you to release immediately, but gives you the assignment to pray about the word prior to its release.

Prophetic ministers (as well as those members desiring to be used prophetically) must learn that their gifting will increase through prayer. They must possess the drive and initiative to pray, pray, and then pray some more.

As we learn to seek the Lord's face through prayer and fervent intercession, we will see an increase in our prophetic anointing and a more accurate release in our gifting.

REFLECTIVE QUESTIONS

1. List the four attributes of a Prophet. For each attribute — what is most important to you?

2. What are the three areas of prayer and intercession that are activated when a person starts to develop their prophetic gifting?

3. True or False?
   _____ All Prophets share the commonality of the call, process and commission.
   _____ God allows the believer to determine if they are a Prophet and lets them appoint themselves to the Office.
   _____ The Bible says to desire the fivefold office.
   _____ During the PIT process, God tries to build your faith.

4. What does Deuteronomy 18:15 (NKJV) say?

5. What does God do to you in the PIT Process?

6. The Purpose of the PIT process is designed to do what?

REFLECTIVE QUESTIONS

7. List seven (7) areas that the PIT process brings forth purity in the Prophet.

8. Why does God call individuals to the Office of the Prophet?

9. Complete this statement: "As a Prophet starts to understand and develop…

10. Why is the purifying process so hard?

RESTORING PROPHETIC INTEGRITY

Dreams and Visions (The Seer Dimension)

Dreams and visions are avenues of pictorial revelation that the Holy Spirit uses to communicate with us. They are closely related in that they speak a message into our lives from the Lord. God regularly speaks to the Prophet through dreams and visions. Numbers 12:6 says, *"If there be a prophet among you, I the Lord God will make Myself know unto him in a vision, and will speak unto him in a dream (KJV)."* Dreams occur during our sleep time and visions often occur while we are fully awake or conscience.

Understanding Dreams and Visions

The word tells us that God has several purposes for dreams and visions that He uses to get His messages across to us. He tells us that dreams and visions:
- Gives us direction – Acts 9:10 and Acts 16:9
- Gives us warnings – Acts 22:17
- Encourages us – Acts 27:23
- Reveal the promises of God to us – Genesis 37:5
- Give us prophetic messages for the future – Luke 1:22

RESTORING PROPHETIC INTEGRITY

God speaks through dreams and vision with the use of the eyes. The eyes are one of the things God uses to give us access to the spirit realm. Prophetically, He wants us to see what He is doing and what He is going to do. It is just as important to see with our spiritual eyes as it is with our natural eyes. John 5:19 indicates that Jesus only did what He saw the Father do. He was referring to what he saw happening in the spirit.

As human beings, we have been trained to operate out of our minds (our soulish realm) and not our spirit. In contrary, as Prophets we cannot live out of our minds. We must live in the spirit and operate out of the spirit.

As Prophets, we must train our eyes to see in the spirit. In order to train our eyes, we must ask the Lord to speak to us when we are awake and when we are sleep. Then we must immediately document what He shows us so we don't lose the detail. This training is developed over time and should become a part of the Prophet's daily discipline regimen.

Categories of Dreams and Visions

Three Levels of Dreams and Visions
Revelation
1) Reveals something about you – Job 33:14-18
2) Reveals something about someone else – Acts 9:10
3) Reveals something that is taking place in the spirit realm – Genesis 28:10-17

Three Main Sources of Dreams and Visions
1) Holy Spirit
2) Soulish realm – infiltration of your subconscious and imagination
3) Demonic – infiltration of your dream world

Three Levels of Vision
1) Dream State – when you doze off in the middle of day and immediately go into a dream
2) Open Visions – full HD color picture in front of you
3) Trance state – the state of altered consciousness (these are rare – Acts 10)

Different Types of Dreams

- Dreams related to purpose – reveal your call, ministry, business or gifts
- Intercessory Dreams – dreams that reveal prayer and intercessory assignments
- Dreams revealing current situations, people, places, cities and nations to pray for
- Warfare Dreams – revealing your fight against powers of darkness – you may be asleep but you are really actively engaged in warfare in the spirit realm
- Warning Dreams –instructions not go a certain place or do a certain thing
- Encouraging Dreams – dreams to encourage you in your walk with Christ, letting you know you are on the right path
- False dreams and vision – inspired by the enemy, to sow confusion, cause your spirit to be at unrest which leaves you feeling faithless, and having fear, doubt and unbelief

RESTORING PROPHETIC INTEGRITY

Dream and Vision Interpretation

The interpretation of dreams and visions is a very complex process. This process consists of diligently seeking the Lord regarding the dreams and visions, and any related details. It also consists of listening to the Holy Spirit to find out what each revelation means.

Three Levels of Dreams and Visions Revelation
1) Personal
2) Church – local assembly, Church of the city, national church, and the Body of Christ
3) Nation(al)

Important Tips for Dream Interpretation
- Ask the Holy Spirit for revelation and insight
- Search for scriptural confirmation
- Know that God will use terms you are familiar with
- Consecutive dreams often have the same message or similar meaning; God may speak the same message more than once

- It is quite possible to have more than one interpretation from one dream (just as it is with scripture). Be open and let the Holy Spirit reveal it to you.

Dream and Vision Journaling

Daniel 7:1 - In the first year of Belshazzar king of Babylon, Daniel had a dream and visions of his head while on his bed. Then he wrote down the dream, telling the main facts (NKJV).

Journaling your dreams and visions allows you to see clearly and define what the Lord is speaking to you. The act of journaling is just as important as receiving The interpretation of the dream itself. Keeping documented details of dreams that you receive over the course of your life can be likened to putting together a 1000 piece puzzle.

RESTORING PROPHETIC INTEGRITY

Suggestions for Journaling Your Dreams and Visions

1. Keep a pen and pad or voice recorder next to your bed, on the floor or a bedside night table.

2. When you first awaken, lay still with your eyes closed and review the dream. Many people who are visually-oriented will often see the dream again prior to recording it.

3. Try to record your dream within the first 10 minutes; this usually allows you to remember more of the dream than recording it later.

4. Start writing or recording the dream just as you remember it. Do not try to write or explain what you think it means. Journal the dream just as you saw it.

5. Document the date and time you had the dream.

RESTORING PROPHETIC INTEGRITY

6. Document important details such as symbols, colors, numbers, people, characters, places, and your feelings and emotions during the dream or vision.

7. Always pray and ask the Lord for understanding and interpretation of the dream. Be patient for the response!

8. Once you receive the interpretation, record it. If you receive an interpretation later, journal that response as well.

9. If you are journaling the dream later than the original time you received it, and you cannot remember the dream in detail, try to remember and journal fragments of the dream that you do remember.

10. Remember to journal as much as you can.

REFLECTIVE QUESTIONS

1. List the five purposes for dreams and visions.

2. What are the three levels of dream and vision revelation?

3. What are the three levels of visions? Describe each.

4. What are the three main sources of dreams?

5. List the different types of dreams.

6. List the different levels of dream and vision interpretation.

7. True or False?
   ___ God will use terms that are familiar to you.
   ___ Ask the Holy Spirit for insight.
   ___ Only one final interpretation will come forth from the dream or vision.

8. Complete the following:
   a) Why is the act of journaling your dreams important?
   b) Daniel 7:1 (NKJV) says. *"In the first year of Belshazzar king of Babylon, Daniel...*

REFLECTIVE QUESTIONS

Review "Suggestions for Journaling Your Dreams and Visions"

Section 3

Restoring Prophetic Integrity

Prophetic Integrity

THERE HAS BEEN MUCH DEFILEMENT IN THE PROPHETIC CAMP. A lot of the purity has been lost. The prophetic gift has been watered down to merely prophesying houses, cars, husbands, wives, money falling from the sky and soliciting payment for a prophetic word. This level of personal prophecy does not even scratch the surface of the truest prophetic dimension. It is only one level of operation.

Prophets must realize that personal prophecy is the lowest level or lowest form of prophecy. Anyone can prophesy warm and fuzzy stuff, but it takes a mantle to shift people, spiritual realms, atmospheres, cities, regions and nations into the will of God.

As we know, the enemy's goal is to defile the Prophets and bring shame to the prophetic gifting. Most of the defilement of the prophetic has been due to a lack of understanding of the office, role and mandate of the Prophet's function. Although the five-fold offices have been restored, there is still much misunderstanding on how to operate and release the gifts and anointing to their full measure. The Lord showed me that a three-dimensional prophetic release is required to establish an accurate prophetic foundation.

The Lord entrusted me with a visual of the prophetic dimension. I was shown a thermometer with three levels. Just as the thermometer has levels that increase with temperature changes, it is the same with the levels of release in the prophetic dimension. The first level is the personal level of prophecy that edifies, exhorts, and comforts.

The second level is intermediate prophecy. It has the ability to unlock an individuals' destiny. From this level we shift people into the plans, purposes and the will of God. The third level of the prophetic is where we shift territories – churches, cities, states and nations into their roles in the kingdom of our Lord and of His Christ. This third level warrants another level of sacrifice from the Prophet because operation on this level is only achieved by the Prophet's mantle and not the prophetic gifting.

RESTORING PROPHETIC INTEGRITY

The Return of Purity

The Lord greatly desires to have purity return to the prophetic dimension, just as He desires the restoration of the prophetic gift as a whole back to the body of Christ. This can be accomplished through proper instruction and training. The Lord is grieved at the state of defilement in the prophetic today. However, because of his loving kindness and his redemptive nature, he always allows restoration to come. Today, as prophetic voices, we have to answer the call and walk in prophetic integrity, not some of the time but all of the time.

Your credibility as a Prophet and or prophetic minister is based solely upon your character and integrity. Although you may be very accurate in your gifting, if your character does not consistently display Christ-like behavior, you run the risk of not being received by your audience because of your behavior.

The enemy has set major traps for Prophets. As noted earlier, one of the enemy's strategies is to defile

Prophets and the prophetic. This is accomplished by causing a disconnect between their lifestyles and their anointing. It is in this mismatch that confusion and deception are released. Due to a lack of true spiritual insight and discernment, many Prophets have fallen into deception. Because Prophets are the mouthpiece of God, it is imperative that they walk the narrow road.

Character Keys to Accuracy and Fruit-filled Prophetic Ministry

Here are a few character keys that will assist Prophets in developing and maintaining prophetic integrity.

Studying the Word of God – It is imperative that every Prophet and prophetic minister study and meditate on the Word of God continuously. *"Study to shew thyself approved unto God, a workman that needeth not to be ashamed, rightly dividing the word of truth (2 Timothy 2:15 – KJV)."* As you process and assimilate the Word of God, it develops a keener sensitivity in the spiritual realm and develops more

RESTORING PROPHETIC INTEGRITY

accuracy. Remember that all revelation, prophecy and spiritual insight must line up with the word of God so it is important to read, meditate and study.

Constantly Seeking the Face of the Lord – As a Prophet, one of your primary responsibilities is to stay in constant communication with the Lord. As you consistently seek the face of God through prayer and ministering to Him through worship, HE will speak to you the mysteries of the kingdom, and give you divine insight into any situation.

Walking in Humility – Every Prophet should walk in humility. Because Prophets have the very nature of Christ, they must not walk puffed up, but walk in a level of humility that honors the Lord (Proverb 16:18-19).

Maintaining a Disciplined Life – As Prophets you MUST maintain a disciplined life. You cannot do all that you want and desire to do. The Lord has put spiritual boundaries around you. My husband and I received a prophetic word from Jim and Carolyn

RESTORING PROPHETIC INTEGRITY

Weiss. The Lord said for us to limit our liberties for the sake of the essence. What the Lord told me and my husband was that some of the liberties that others have, we had to limit because of the essence, which is his Glory. 1 Corinthians 10:23 tells us that all things are lawful but they are not necessarily edifying. There are some things you just cannot do because others are doing them, because your prophetic anointing is at stake.

Walking Upright Before God – Every Prophet and prophetic minister has to live a Godly lifestyle and walk upright before God. This mean that you are to lay aside everything that will cause your walk with God to be jeopardized. *"Therefore we also, since we are surrounded by so great a cloud of witnesses, let us lay aside every weight, and the sin which so easily ensnares us, and let us run with endurance the race that is set before us. – (Hebrews 12:1)."*

Avoid the seven deadly sins and works of the flesh Galatians 5:19): pride, covetousness, lust, gluttony, anger, envy and sloth. This will ensure that your

RESTORING PROPHETIC INTEGRITY

Christian walk and prophetic lifestyle is upright before the Lord.

Walking in Love – If you do not continually walk in the spirit of love, then you will not prophesy in the redemptive nature that Christ came to demonstrate through the cross, which is love. Remember the Spirit of Prophecy is the testimony of Jesus. Jesus came to earth because of the great love the Father had for us. When we prophesy, we should be prophesying out of a pure heart of love, not of critical or judgmental spirits.

Prophetic Purity – The goal of every believer is to grow in sanctification and purity, even more so those who minister prophetically. *Psalm 51:7 says. "Purge me with hyssop, and I shall be clean; Wash me, and I shall be whiter than snow.* Issues of the flesh, unrestrained emotions, soulish desires and sin can all interfere with the line of communication with the Holy Spirit and hinder the release of the prophetic word.

RESTORING PROPHETIC INTEGRITY

Prophets and prophetic ministers desiring to move in deeper levels of the prophetic should seek the Lord for personal deliverance, inner healing, purification and sanctification in every area of their lives. Even though this work is generally obtained through the Lord's process, the prophetic unction may occur before the total process is complete. In other words, one may still be able to prophesy accurately, and still need more purification.

Understanding Timing in Prophetic Release – Understanding and discerning the proper timing to release a prophetic word or utterance is very important. As a Prophet, one should always be so in tune with the Holy Spirit to know when and when not to release a word. Ecclesiastes 5:2 says, "Do not be rash with your mouth, and do not let your heart utter anything hastily before God." This scripture can be applied to the prophetic dimension.

When we receive words from the Lord while in service or in our time of prayer, we have to discern, pray, ask and wait for the appropriate time to release the word.

RESTORING PROPHETIC INTEGRITY

There are times when you receive a word from the Lord and He says not to release it, but to just pray the word through. There could be any number of reasons why this may happen. The hearer may not be in the proper spiritual state to receive the word, or the Lord may have given you a prayer request.

Prophesy ONLY what God has spoken – This is a very important point and is one of the main reasons the prophetic has gotten a bad reputation over the years. There have been Prophets who have spoken what they wanted God to do versus what God is really saying. In Jeremiah 28 we see that Hananiah prophesied what he wanted the Lord to do regarding the children of Israel's Babylonian captivity. Initially, Jeremiah cosigned this prophecy. During his personal time the Lord corrected Jeremiah. He had to go back and prophesy to Hananiah because Hananiah erred. The lesson: **only** prophesy what the Lord has spoken, and not be zealous for God to do something else.

RESTORING PROPHETIC INTEGRITY

Fasting – Prophets should develop a lifestyle of fasting to maintain constant and consistent open communication. Fasting keeps the spirit in tune with God at all times. When Prophets fast, they exercise fleshly restraints for the sake of prophetic accuracy (Daniel9:3-4; Luke 2:37).

No Compromise – Compromise leads to contamination. Prophets cannot compromise the word of the Lord in any way, shape, or form. If you compromise on any level it will contaminate your prophetic anointing. If a Prophet gets contaminated, they will be ineffective and hindered in completing their assignment. In Daniel 1:8-9, we see that Daniel did not compromise when it came to the king's delicacies but honored his relationship with God.

RESTORING PROPHETIC INTEGRITY

Prophetic Contaminants

Contaminants to the Prophetic Release

As the release of the prophetic is being restored, the prophetic minister must understand what could contaminate the receiving and releasing of prophetic words from the Lord. The enemy fights hard to deflect God's instructions from those chosen to release the prophetic gifting. It is here that He unleashes all that He has to keep the Word of the Lord from being released. DO NOT allow these hindrances to stop you from releasing what God is speaking in this prophetic hour.

Below is a list of common contaminants:

Fear — If you have any level of fear or those in the service are fearful, it can hinder the release. Fear paralyzes the believer and causes them to shut down.

> *2 Timothy 1:7 (NKJV) – "For God has not given us a spirit of fear, but of power and of love and of a sound mind."*

RESTORING PROPHETIC INTEGRITY

Sin and Lack of Deliverance — Sin and the lack of deliverance keeps an open door for the spirit of divination; obvious and not so obvious. Sin on any level will contaminate the Word of the Lord.

> *Romans 6:12 (AMP) – "Let not sin therefore rule as king in your mortal short-lived, (perishable) bodies, to make you yield to its cravings and be subject to its lusts and evil passions."*

Intimidation — This contaminant can be just as paralyzing as fear. If you are intimidated by other Prophets, perhaps because they have been in prophetic ministry longer than you, it could hinder the prophetic release).

> *Philippians 1:6 (AMP) – "And I am convinced and sure of this very thing, that He Who began a good work in you will continue until the day of Jesus time of His return], developing [that good work] and bringing it to full completion in you."*

RESTORING PROPHETIC INTEGRITY

Ignorance — When God gives you a prophetic word, do not be wise in your own eyes, but ask the Lord for wisdom. For example, the Lord gives you a prophetic word and tells you that a person is going to walk again. You go and tell a person in a wheelchair whose legs are covered with a blanket that they are going to walk. Then you pull the blanket off and they don't even have legs. That's a fleshly misinterpretation of what you heard from the Lord. Do not be presumptuous in interpreting the word that you are given. Use wisdom. Ignorance is not bliss, it is a curse!

> *James 1:5 (AMP)* – *"If any of you is deficient in wisdom, let him ask of the giving God [Who gives] to everyone liberally and ungrudgingly, without reproaching or faultfinding, and it will be given him."*

Rebellion and Disobedience — This is very important as some Prophets don't even realize they are in rebellion and disobedience. In the simplest form, if God tells you to prophesy and you decide not to, you are disobedient. If God tells you NOT to prophesy and you continue prophesying, not obeying the Lord, you are in rebellion. Rebellion and disobedience will almost always shut the Prophets' hearing and communication with the Lord off.

> *1 Samuel 15:22-23-22 (NKJV)* – *"Has the Lord as great delight in burnt offerings and sacrifices, As in obeying the voice of the Lord? Behold, to obey is better than sacrifice, And to heed than the fat of rams. For rebellion is as the sin of witchcraft, And stubbornness is as iniquity and idolatry. Because you have rejected the word of the Lord, He also has rejected you from being King."*

Pride – Haughty and prideful prophetic people will always have a great fall. God will shut off your hearing if you are prideful. However, DO NOT get confidence and boldness in the Holy Spirit misconstrued as pride. Your discernment will let you know when a person's behavior is prideful.

When a prophetic minister humbles himself, God gives him more grace to minister prophetically.

RESTORING PROPHETIC INTEGRITY

Pride cont'd

> *Proverbs 16:18-19- 18 (NKJV)* — *"Pride goes before destruction, And a haughty spirit before a fall. Better to be of a humble spirit with the lowly, than to divide the spoil with the proud."*
>
> *James 4:6 (NKJV)* – *"God resists the proud, but give grace to the humble."*

Impure Intentions of the Heart — Prophets who prophesy with wrong motives and only use the prophetic to elevate themselves and to advance their personal ministry are not walking in prophetic integrity. As Prophets, we have to always do heart checks and make sure our intentions are pure and there is no other motive than God's and that is to turn the hearts of the sons back to the Father.

RESTORING PROPHETIC INTEGRITY

> *Hebrews 4:12-13 (NKJV) – "For the word of God is living and powerful, and sharper than any two-edged sword, piercing even to the division of soul and spirit, and of joints and marrow, and is a discerner of the thoughts and intents of the heart. And there is no creature hidden from His sight, but all things are naked and open to the eyes of Him to whom we must give account."*

This is very dangerous because if a Prophet is not completely healed, they will prophesy out of that hurt and bitterness. Typically, this is why a lot of Prophets are very judgmental in their delivery style and do not flow in the redemptive nature of Christ. The Lord instructed us to forgive those who have wronged us. So forgive and keep it moving!

> *Matthew 18:21-22- 21 (NKJV) — "Then Peter came to Him and said, "Lord, how often shall my brother sin against me, and I forgive him? Up to seven times?" Jesus said to him, I do not say to you, up to seven times. But up to seventy times seven."*

RESTORING PROPHETIC INTEGRITY

Uncontrolled or Untamed Tongue — An untamed tongue will go forth in lying, exaggerating, gossiping and cursing. A Prophet must learn to tame their tongue because they will release either life or death when they speak. A lying tongue cannot release an accurate word from the Lord. Pray and ask the Lord to take the coals from the altar of God and cleanse your tongue.

> *James 2:6 (NKJV) – "And the tongue is a fire, a world of iniquity. The tongue is so set among our members that it defiles the whole body and sets on fire the course of nature; and it is set on fire by hell."*

> *Proverbs 12:22 (NKJV) – "Lying lips are an abomination to the Lord, But those who deal truthfully are His delight.*

Uncontrollable desires — Any and all addictions or uncontrollable desires can get in the way of hearing clearly from the Lord. For example, I love to watch movies and especially reality TV shows, but if I commit to watching too much of those type of shows or movies, they could cloud my hearing from the Lord.

> *Romans 6:12 (AMP) – Let not sin therefore rule as king in your mortal (short-lived, perishable) bodies, to make you yield to its cravings and be subject to its lusts and evil passions.*

Anger — Have you ever seen a Prophet and their face is all flinched up and they say I am in the spirit, don't touch me or talk to me before I minister or prophesy." Some Prophets have an angry, demonic spirit and try to mask it as being deep. This is total foolishness. You don't have to be mean and rude and pretend to be deep. Let the love of God rule and guide your heart. Whatever is in your heart will come out when you prophesy. Any level of anger can cause you to not hear the Lord.

> *Proverbs 29:22 – "An angry man stirs up strife, And a furious man abounds in transgression."*

RESTORING PROPHETIC INTEGRITY

Humanism — This is the promotion of human logic, nature, understanding, knowledge, wisdom or common sense above the wisdom of God. A Prophet should not include earthly wisdom in their prophetic release. You should never exalt worldly information over God's wisdom and His word. As a Prophet, you can shift atmospheres and because of this, you do not want to mix humanistic viewpoints and new age ideologies with the word of the Lord.

> *James 3:14-17 (NKJV) – "But if you have bitter envy and self-seeking in your hearts, do not boast and lie against the truth. This wisdom does not descend from above, but is earthly, sensual, demonic. For where envy and self-seeking exist, confusion and every evil thing are there. But the wisdom that is from above is first pure, then peaceable, gentle, willing to yield, full of mercy and good fruits, without partiality and without hypocrisy.*

These words are worthy of repeating: DO NOT allow these hindrances to stop you from releasing what God is speaking in this prophetic hour.

RESTORING PROPHETIC INTEGRITY

Checks & Balances of Prophetic Ministry

Checks and Balances of the Prophetic Words

One area of the prophetic dimension that has been lacking is that of judging prophetic words. This is largely due to a lack of prophetic protocol and a lack of understanding on the part of the body. This is because judging prophetic words is subject to error.

Scripture tells us that we know in part; therefore, we can only prophesy in part and not the whole. Personal prophecy must be judged and tested prior to acting on it (1 Corinthians 13:9).

> *1 Corinthians 14:29 – "Let two or three prophets speak, and let the others judge."*

Do not test the word based on your personal suspicions. Just because a Prophet is typically accurate does not exclude them from this test. Their prophetic word should still be tested according to 1 Thessalonians 5-21 which says "Test all things; hold fast what is good."

RESTORING PROPHETIC INTEGRITY

The following guidelines can be used as a checklist for judging prophecy. It is not all-inclusive; it's merely a guide.

Scriptural Validity — First you have to ask yourself if the prophetic word you received lines up with scripture (2 Corinthians 13:8). Prophetic words should always align with the word of God. Because prophecy is the testimony of Jesus Christ, the word should bear witness with Christ, and it must bear witness with the receiver (John 16:13-14). Take an evaluation of the prophetic word. Does the word glorify and reveal Christ (the *"Christos,"* the anointing), or does it glorify the person giving the word?

The prophetic word should give God glory and not grief. The primary focus of the prophetic word should be to edify, exhort and comfort (1 Corinthians 14:3). Even in an open rebuke, there is a level of building and planting. God does not come to scatter, He comes to gather!

RESTORING PROPHETIC INTEGRITY

Prophetic Manipulation — There may be times when a Prophet can prophesy and attempt to control you or manipulate you through their false word and the use of scripture. This typically happens when the Prophet wants you to do what they want you to do, versus doing what God wants. The error comes when the directive is something other than what God has spoken to you. You must use discernment to know when this is happening. Hearing the word of the Prophet is different than being forced or coerced to hear the word of the Prophet.

God told the young Prophet to do one thing. The old Prophet told the young Prophet to do something different. The old Prophet was not a false Prophet, yet he told the young Prophet to do something that resulted in him disobeying the word of God, even though he (the older Prophet) told him to do it. The key is to be OBEDIENT to the Lord in all things.

When you are receiving a prophetic word, there should be some level of confirmation that bears witness in your spirit. The word should leap in you

RESTORING PROPHETIC INTEGRITY

and resonate in your spirit (Romans 8:16). Those who are mature in the Lord hear and know His voice.

Misdirection — The spirit of Jezebel will give prophetic words to lead people astray. They will say things like, "you do not need to hear from anyone but me." They will also say, "do not let anyone pray for you but me" and "I am true Prophet, listen to me." This spirit will also use prophecy to seduce you away from leadership and cause chaos in the local body (1 John 4:1, 1 Thessalonians 5:12, Deuteronomy 13:1-5).

In Deuteronomy 18:22, the Lord is telling us that if the word of the Prophet does not come to pass, then the word of prophecy was not from Him. However, we are not talking about an impatient person's time frame, where they want it to happen right away. It may be years before some prophetic words come to pass. For example, when Samuel anointed David as king and prophesied to him, David did not begin his reign at eight years old when he was anointed. The word took years to manifest.

It is important to also mention that prophetic words are conditional. There are some things you may need to do in order for the prophetic word to come to pass. The best example is if you get a prophetic word that you are going to the nations and you never get your passport, then the Prophet wasn't a false Prophet. The word didn't come to pass as predicted because you didn't take proper action on the word and get your passport.

When you receive a prophetic word it should be refreshing to you. When you receive a prophetic word, it should bring you peace and produce a level of fruitfulness (Colossians 3:15). It should never leave you confused and not knowing what to do. God is not the author of confusion. The prophetic word will produce freedom and not bondage.

Instability in the Prophetic Dimension

Instability can be defined as having a lack of stable emotions or mental stability. As stated previously, if you are living in the soulish realm, your emotions are not subject to the Holy Spirit. Therefore, when you

RESTORING PROPHETIC INTEGRITY

speak, you will release a word from the soulish realm and not from the spirit of God. Thus, you are prophesying out of the emotional or soulish realm.

Due to the instability of the prophetic, there is truly a need for teaching and training. This instability is the root cause for the prophetic dimension not being released in the modern day church. Pastors and leaders in the Body of Christ have been bruised, burnt, stabbed, betrayed and manipulated by unstable and immature prophetic people. These unstable and immature Prophets and those called to the prophetic ministry have given the prophetic a bad rap. Listed below are some things that have caused instability in the prophetic dimension.

Lack of Submission – One of the primary issues with Prophets is they think they can operate in a Christ centered dimension without submission. Although one would be able to prophesy, proper submission to an apostolic anointing will keep balance in a Prophet's life.

RESTORING PROPHETIC INTEGRITY

An Unteachable Spirit — There are Prophets who presume to know everything and you and no one else can tell them anything. The classic line goes, "I hear from God so you can't tell me anything." This mentality is skating on thin ice. A Prophet can always learn something, no matter how mature you are in your gifting. Most seasoned Prophets still look to learn and glean from other Prophets and prophetic ministers.

Absence of purification – When there is an absence of purification in the life of a Prophet; they run the risk of defilement and contamination. If they reject the process and formation work of Christ in their life, their words are empty and leave the receiver feeling voided.

Soulish Realm – Prophesying out of this realm is very dangerous. When you are ruled or governed by your emotions or are very analytical, you run the risk of trying to interpret the word God gave you. Also, when your emotions are fragmented, you release a fragmented word of confusion.

RESTORING PROPHETIC INTEGRITY

Spirit of Divination — Divination is the act of obtaining secret knowledge about a person or situation, especially that which relates to the future or future events. Obtaining this information outside of the Holy Spirit constitutes divination and witchcraft.

> *John 10:1 — "Most assuredly, I say to you, he who does not enter the sheepfold by the door, but climbs up some other way, the same is a thief and a robber."*

It is easy to tap into this spirit and operate outside of it IF you do not study the word of God, have a prayer life and fail to walk in integrity. If your lifestyle is not a Godly one, you will fall into divination and not even know it.

> *Leviticus 20:27 — "A man or a woman who is a medium, or who has familiar spirits, shall surely be put to death; they shall stone them with stones. Their blood shall be upon them."*

RESTORING PROPHETIC INTEGRITY

Prophesying when God has not spoken – ONLY SPEAK WHAT GOD SAYS TO SPEAK!!! Prophets should not make up or release false prophetic words to seem like they are a "super-Prophet." This not only endangers the Prophet, but it causes confusion in the receivers' life.

> *Deuteronomy 18:20 – "But the prophet who presumes to speak a word in my name, which I have not commanded him to speak, or who speaks in the name of other gods, that prophet shall die."*

The Hurt Prophet – Hurt Prophets and prophetic ministers hurt other people. Hurt Prophets emerge when true forgiveness has not taken place, and one has not allowed the Lord to fight their battles. Hurt prophetic people usually isolate themselves from other parts of the body. In the meantime, when they minister, they inevitably hurt other people. The root cause of this hurt usually stems from either their gifting being stifled, shut down, or by them being REJECTED by those whom they thought would

RESTORING PROPHETIC INTEGRITY

receive them.

Most Prophets and prophetic ministers, when hurt, fight to prove they have a prophetic gifting and that God speaks to them. You should NEVER have to fight or force anyone to believe that you are a true Prophet. YOUR FRUIT will speak for you. Deal with any rejection that may be lying dormant from previous church relationships. Prophets have a tendency to walk and prophesy out of that hurt and rejection and thus drive the nails of rejection into an even deeper hole that only Christ can fill.

False Prophets — In the Old Testament the Lord was grieved by the false Prophets. In Jeremiah 23, the Lord deals harshly with false Prophets. In Jeremiah 23:14 he says, *"Also I have seen a horrible thing in the prophets of Jerusalem: They commit adultery and walk in lies; They also strengthen the hands of evildoers, So that no one turns back from his wickedness. All of them are like Sodom to Me, and her inhabitants like Gomorrah."* In the New Testament, 1 John 4:1 talks about false Prophets amongst you. It is the same today. (See 2 Peter 2:1-2 and Matthew 7:15:16).

Initial Signs of a False Prophet
- The false Prophet will prophesy when God has not spoken (Deuteronomy 18:20).
- A false Prophet will prophesy false visions not from he Lord but demonic entities (Jeremiah 23:32).
- A false Prophet will prophesy only what you want to hear and what makes you feel good.
- A false Prophet will prophesy and the word will not come to pass.
- A true Prophet can become a false Prophet by allowing the pressures of people pulling on or resisting the mantle. For example, a person can start out as a true Prophet but because of self-recognition and a need for acceptance, he or she can become false.

Prophetic Protocol – Prophets and Apostles
The relationship between Apostles and Prophets are imperative. As noted in Ephesians 3:20, they are the

RESTORING PROPHETIC INTEGRITY

foundation of the Church. Together with Elders, they are considered foundational ministries of a local assembly and the Church of a particular city or region. Apostles and Prophets give balance to one another because they are complimentary ministry gifts. As Apostles build the vision of God, Prophets hear detailed instructions from God and communicate them to the Apostle. Prophets in turn need the Apostles to bring governmental order in their lives.

I was in a service where Jim Goll was ministering and he stated that, "Prophets without Apostles is like a helium balloon without a string." In essence, he is saying prophetic people can wander off into dimensions they are not called to or are not ready to encounter. This order is not to restrict the Prophet in any means, but serves as positive affirmation of the prophetic grace upon a Prophet's life, releasing them into their destinies. Every Prophet and prophetic minister needs apostolic balance in their life.

Prophetic Protocol – Pastors and Prophets

This section will touch on Prophets and how they work in conjunction to leaders, and their other fivefold office counterparts. My husband (who functions as an Apostle) and I (functioning as a Prophet) have seen and heard many encounters regarding flakey,

RESTORING PROPHETIC INTEGRITY

self-appointed Prophets. They have caused utter chaos in the local church by not submitting to authority, prophesying falsely, causing church splits, dividing the church and scattering the sheep. This behavior is a result of immature prophetic people who have perhaps had little to no ministerial training.

Unfortunately, these prophetic individuals blame Pastors for shutting their gift down or quenching their spirit if they have a word or God has spoken something to them. Some prophetic people think that submission to authority is the equivalent of a church "swear" word. This is a major cause for Pastors and other five-fold leaders not readily receiving the prophetic community. However, this is changing. God is raising the bar for Prophets and those who minister prophetically.

It is vitally important for Prophets and Pastors to work together, just as it is for Apostles and Prophets, Evangelist and Prophets and Teachers and Prophets. The prophetic gifting is vital to the other four, just as the other four are vital to the Prophet. Prophets must

RESTORING PROPHETIC INTEGRITY

understand this. Since Prophets will be raised up in the local house, or sent out to minister in other local assemblies, it is important for them to understand protocol from a pastoral perspective. Pastors are shepherds and they are going to protect the sheep at any cost. Prophets must have an understanding of this and know that it is not the goal of every Pastor to shut them down and not release the prophetic gifting.

Now if the prophetic individual or Prophet has been suspect in their relationship, service and commitment to the local body, your fruit will be questioned. However, I am not speaking to the controlling Pastors who want to control the gifting of the Prophets, but to the Prophets.

My desire is to provide some guidelines for protocol that will help alleviate some — if not all — of the misconceptions that exist. Moreover, there are a number of Pastors who understand, welcome and receive Prophets to come in and minister what the Lord is saying. Remember, your gift will make room for you and bring you before great men. You don't

RESTORING PROPHETIC INTEGRITY

have to force, push or pull a Pastor to allow you to minister in their church. When it is God's set-time, the doors will swing wide before you.

Prophetic Protocol Prophets and Prophetic Ministers

The basic guidelines listed below are for the purpose of maintaining order in the house. It is designed for Prophets and prophetic ministers. It is general by design, since each local assembly will have different guidelines for releasing the prophetic. You should always check with the Pastors or leaders of the house to get permission for releasing the prophetic word, vision, prophetic impressions, etc.

1. **Always record your prophecies**. Record prophecies by using a tape, CD, cell phone or transcription. Documentation will eliminate any misunderstanding and misinterpretation of the word in the future. This is for the protection of the prophetic minister giving the word, and for the person receiving the word as well. Your recorded prophecies can also serve as a weapon to release in times when

you are challenged in your walk. Continually listening to your prophetic word increases your faith, even if its months or years down the line.

2. **Prophecies should be submitted to local authority.** Prophecies that are received by other prophetic gifts in the Body of Christ should always be given and reviewed by your Pastors, even if they are not currently moving in the prophetic dimension. Although they (Pastors) might not understand the prophetic, the word will help them understand you better.

3. **Submit your word to the leadership of the local assembly.** This will assure the timing is correct. If you are one who gets angry when leadership tells you the word is not for the congregation, or it is not time to release the word, then you'll need to check your heart and your motives. Remember, leadership is given to help you continue to grow and mature in your gifting. YOU have to be able to take the NOT RIGHT NOW responses and ALWAYS maintain a teachable spirit (1 Corinthians 14:32).

4. **Prophets minister to the local body.** The prophetic ministry is first in the local church, then abroad. Although you may have a ministry to the nations, your prophetic ministry should be developed, nurtured and released in the local church. Once God sees you are faithful in serving at home, then He will open doors for ministry abroad.

5. **House Prophets.** Prophets who are reared in the local church become pillars in the house of God. They use their gifts to build and grow the house of God.

6. **Accountability.** This word has become a forbidden word in the mouth of Prophets and prophetic ministers who have been hurt. There should be no long rangers in the body, especially in the prophetic dimension because we each have a part of the puzzle. Therefore, accountability is imperative for Prophets and prophetic ministers.

Accountability warrants covering, protection, growth and launching into dimensions the enemy is seeking to devour. When Prophets and prophetic ministers

RESTORING PROPHETIC INTEGRITY

have no accountability, it is like being in the rain without an umbrella, and the rain storms of life will drench you.

Wisdom Keys for Restoring Prophetic Integrity

- Always submit to authority
- Maintain a teachable spirit
- Always prophesy in the spirit of love
- Avoid lecturing and whipping people with prophecy
- Avoid prophesying your favorite words
- Stick to the word that God has given you; do not add or take away from it
- Stay within your measure of faith
- DO NOT prophesy if you have an unclear message; meaning if your word is not clear to you it will cause confusion to the hearer, church or nation
- DO NOT mix your personal problems into your prophetic words
- Always stay in tune with the Spirit of God and the flow of the service
- Refrain from always prophesying redundant and repetitive words

RESTORING PROPHETIC INTEGRITY

- Avoid correcting leadership through prophetic words publicly
- Never feel pressured to prophesy a lengthy word if you don't have one
- Never allow your prophetic gift to replace God in a person's life
- Never use prophetic words to exert authority in a person's life
- Never use prophetic words to control or manipulate others

REFLECTIVE QUESTIONS

1. List the character keys to accuracy and fruit-filled prophetic ministry.

2. Which of the Prophetic Contaminants are most important to you and why?

3. What are some of guides for judging prophecy?

4. List the things that have caused instability in the prophetic dimension as mentioned in this section.

5. Finish these Statements:
   Hurt Prophets and ...
   Hurt Prophets fight ...

6. List the initial signs of a false prophet

7. Out of the 12 Wisdom Keys, what are the six which speak to you the loudest (or mean the most)?

REFLECTIVE QUESTIONS

8. Fill in the blanks. Your word choices are below:

eliminate	record	nations	prophetic
misunderstanding	released	challenges	Prophets
developed	misinterpretation	weapon	nurtured
accountability	build	grow	grounded
Apostles	covering	growth	Protection and Launching

a. Always _____ a prophetic word so that you will _____ any _____ and _____ of the word.

b. Recorded prophecies serve as a _____ in times of _____ in your walk with Christ.

c. Although you may have a ministry to the _____, your _____ ministry should be _____, _____, and _____ in the local church.

d. _____ use their gifts to _____ and _____ the house of God.

REFLECTIVE QUESTIONS

e. _____ is imperative for Prophets, it warrants _____, _____, _____ and _____ into a dimension the enemy is seeking to devour.

f. Prophets needs _____ to keep them _____.

Section 4

Mandate, Mantle & Mission

The Mandate, Mantle and Mission

EVERY PROPHET HAS BEEN GIVEN A MANDATE, A MANTLE AND A MISSION. The mandate (assignment) is a God-given assignment the Prophet is to carry out until its completion. The mantle (the power) is the embodiment of the prophetic dimension of the Christos operating within the individual. The mission (how the assignment is carried out) is the design God will use for the Prophet to fulfill the mandate.

When a Prophet is called, a mandate, mantle and mission is given from the Lord to the Office of Prophet. The discovery and execution of the mandate, mantle and mission is manifested at the time of commissioning. For example, as a Prophet to the nation, the mantle gives you the power and authority to speak to kings, presidents and leaders world-wide. The mandate, mantle and mission determine the particular nations you go to and the sphere of influence you have while there.

RESTORING PROPHETIC INTEGRITY

Identifying and Understanding Your Mandate

It is important for Prophets to know how to identify and understand their mandate. Some of you may already know your mandate and others may not. If there is any uncertainty regarding your mandate, begin to fervently seek the Lord for clarification and instruction regarding your call. You'll want to commit to fulfilling the mandated assignment the Lord gives you. Once there is clarification of the mandate then seek the Lord for instructions to carry it out.

Indicate your mandate here:

_____

_____

_____

_____

_____

_____

_____

_____

A Historical Look at Old Testament and New Testament Prophets

The Prophets of the Old Testament were broken down into three categories. The first two categories were based upon the writings of what is known as the "major" and "minor" Prophets. These terms "major" and "minor" Prophets are not referring to their significance or the mantle that was upon their lives. These terms are merely a reference to the length of what was attributed to their writings.

These two types of Prophets' assignments were to turn the hearts of their audience back to God. In the process, some of them prophesied against God's people and pronounced judgments, exiles, and restoration. Others, such as Jonah, Joel and Hosea spoke words of prophecy that declared God's love to all mankind – not just his chosen people Israel. Each of these Prophets was God's mouthpiece revealing the destiny of His beloved. Let's take a look at the Major and Minor Prophets. Please note, their names were tied to their purpose.

RESTORING PROPHETIC INTEGRITY

Major Prophets and Their Purpose

Isaiah – The name Isaiah means, "Yahweh is Salvation." His very name denoted the message he was to give to Israel. His ministry's purpose was to call the nation of Judah back to God and to tell them of God's salvation through the coming Christ.

Jeremiah – Jeremiah means, "Jehovah has appointed." His name speaks to the fact that he was chosen by God before he was in his mother's womb to carry a message of repentance to Judah and insist they turn from their sins and back to God (Jeremiah 1:1-11).

Ezekiel – Ezekiel means, "God Strengthens." His purpose was to announce God's judgment on Israel and other nations which would bring God's future blessing and strengthen His covenant with His people.

Daniel – Daniel means, "God is My Judge." His name reveals his purpose of consecration to Yahweh and subsequently the restoration of God's covenant to Israel.

RESTORING PROPHETIC INTEGRITY

Minor Prophets and Their Purpose

Hosea – Hosea means, "Salvation or Deliverance." His purpose was to demonstrate Gods unconditional love for His bride.

Joel – Joel means, "Yahweh is God." His purpose was to urge Judah to return to God before impending judgment. Also, He spoke of the outpouring of the Holy Spirit before the great and awesome day of the Lord.

Amos – Amos means, "Burden-Bearer." His purpose was to pronounce God's judgment upon Israel, the nations and Prophets who error in their ways.

Obadiah – Obadiah means, "Servant or Worshiper of Yahweh." Obadiah brings the message of assurance that God will intervene and restore His people as well as punish those who have harmed them.

Jonah – Jonah means, "Dove or Pigeon." Jonah was to show the extent of God's grace and mercy to all who would turn to Him.

Micah – Micah means, "Who is like Yahweh." His name speaks of God's great compassion to forgive the sins of all mankind.

Nahum – Nahum means, "Comforter or Full of Comfort." His message was to declare that God would comfort Judah during Assyrian judgment.

Habakkuk – Habakkuk means, "Embrace." His name speaks to the message that God will embrace those who put their faith in Him.

Zephaniah – Zephaniah means, "The Lord Has Hidden." His primary message was to declare that there is a remnant that God has hidden under the blood.

Haggai – Haggai means, "Festive." He was to encourage the people of God to rebuild the temple with gladness.

Zechariah – Zechariah means, "Yahweh Remembers." His purpose was to give hope to God's people by revealing God's future deliverance through Jesus Christ the Messiah.

RESTORING PROPHETIC INTEGRITY

Malachi – Malachi means, "My Messenger." His name speaks of the truth that he was God's last messenger before the 450 year silence preceding the announcement of the birth of Christ.

The third type of Old Testament Prophet was not considered a Prophet because of their writings but because of their function. These types of Prophets served as seers, Prophets to kings, watchmen, law givers and judges.

Other Types of Old Testament Prophets

Moses – Prophet and Lawgiver. Writer of the Mosaic Law; The Pentateuch (the first five books of the Bible). (Genesis, Exodus, Leviticus, Numbers, Deuteronomy); (Exodus – Deuteronomy).

Samuel – Israel's last judge; he served as a Prophet and priest. He anointed the first two kings of Israel (1 Samuel 1).

Elijah – considered one of the most powerful Prophets. Show down at Mt. Carmel (1 Kings 17 & 19).

RESTORING PROPHETIC INTEGRITY

Elisha – Elijah's successor who received a double portion of Elijah's mantle (1 Kings 19).

Nathan – Served as a Prophet to King David (2 Samuel 7:2).

Gad – Served as a seer to King David (2 Samuel 24:11).

Ahijah – Prophet during the time of the fall of King Solomon and the reign of Jeroboam (1 King 11).

Jehu – Jehu the son of Hanani, Prophet who prophesied against Baasha (1 King 16).

Micaiah – Prophet who prophesied against Ahab (1 Kings 22).

Shemaiah – Prophet who prophesied against Rehoboam (2 Chronicles 12).

Oded – Prophet who caused Asa to remove idols (2 Chronicles 15).

RESTORING PROPHETIC INTEGRITY

Hanniah – False prophet (Jeremiah 28).

Deborah – Prophetess and only female Judge of Israel (Judges 4:4).

Miriam – Prophetess, sister of Moses (Exodus 15:20).

Huldah – Prophetess, wife of Shallum, keeper of the wardrobe (2 Kings 22:14).

Noadiah – Prophetess worked against Nehemiah (Nehemiah 6:14).

Company of Prophets – (1 Samuel 10:10; 1 Samuel 19:20; 1 Kings 20:35; and 2 Kings 2:3, 5, 7, 15).

As stated before, each of the third types of Prophets (other than Moses) did not write any canonized scripture. Their purpose and assignment was just as important as those who did as it was recorded in the Bible.

New Testament Prophets and Their Purpose

Although the New Testament primarily reveals the ministry of the Apostle, there are several references that speak about Prophets and prophetic people within the New Covenant. In the book of Acts, the church at Antioch had both Prophets and teachers there (Acts 13:1). Also, Ephesians 2:19-20 reveals that the household of God (Church) was built upon the foundations of both the Apostles and Prophets, with Jesus being the Chief Cornerstone.

New Testament Prophets

John the Baptist – Although John the Baptist was in the New Testament, he was considered an Old Testament Prophet. He was assigned to call God's people to repentance and to prepare the way of the Lord. Both Isaiah and Malachi declared that God would send the Prophet Elijah. It was fulfilled through John the Baptist. He was responsible for transitioning Israel from the Law of Moses (Old Testament) to the dispensation of grace (New Testament) through Jesus Christ (Isaiah 40:3; Malachi 4:5).

RESTORING PROPHETIC INTEGRITY

Anna the Prophetess – Anna would be considered an intercessory Prophet. It is recorded that she prayed and fasted in the Temple until the Messiah came (Luke 2:36-38). By ministering in the Temple in this fashion, Anna would also be considered an Old Testament Prophet.

Phillip's Daughters – Acts 21:9 states Philip the Evangelist had four daughters who prophesied. They were not called Prophets by name. But, an interesting note states that they were recorded with the ability to prophesy and were around when Agabus the Prophet came down from Judah (Acts 21:8-10).

Agabus – Agabus was recorded in scripture as having a very accurate gifting. As a Prophet he prophesied the famine that took place throughout the world (Acts 11:28). He also prophesied to the Apostle Paul that he would be bound when he goes to Jerusalem (Acts 21:10-11).

The Prophets at Antioch – There's not much mentioned in scripture about this company of

Prophets other than they spent time worshiping, praying and fasting within the church at Antioch. Their individual names are not recorded, however in conjunction with Ephesians 2:20; 4:11, we understand their role was an important part of God's plan for establishing the Church. See Acts 13:1-3.

Functions of a Mantled (Commissioned) Prophet

As a Prophet is mantled with power, there are certain functions that will be evident in their prophetic ministry. Because Prophets are in constant communication with God, they operate and function in a variety of ways.

Every Prophet has a mandate and a primary message that he has to carry out and deliver. God anoints Prophets to be able to receive the revelation of that word and then endow them with the power to release that word. If you do not know the primary message God is speaking for you to release, you should begin

RESTORING PROPHETIC INTEGRITY

seeking Him fervently so you can be aligned to release his word and fulfill your mandate.

Each Prophet has a sphere of influence that gives him authority in order to impact the spiritual climate of the region, city, state, or nation. This delegated authority allows the Prophets to be effective in the mandate in which they were sent. This is a special grace that is upon Prophets to change atmospheres so breakthroughs can come forth on behalf of an individual, family, church, city, region, state, country and nation.

These functions include but are not limited to:

Moving in Authority – Prophets operate in a level of delegated authority that causes spiritual shifts in atmospheres that releases heaven on earth. This authority is fueled by faith in God. In Joshua 10:13, Joshua moved in authority so much that God heeded his voice and caused the sun and moon to stand still. Prophets today have been given the same level of authority in the spirit realm.

RESTORING PROPHETIC INTEGRITY

Weighty Responsibility – Prophets should not take their call and responsibility lightly. Wearing a Prophet's mantle is a VERY weighty responsibility. This adds great importance to the PURIFYING process. Training prepares the Prophet to carry the weight of the anointing. Otherwise, they would buckle or breakdown from the extreme weight of the mantle.

It cannot be stressed enough: mantles carry weighty responsibilities for individuals, families, cities, and nations. This is not about the Prophet; it is all about Jesus and those God has sent the Prophet to for ministry.

Every Old and New Testament Prophet understood the weightiness of the mantle. That's why they begged, cried and gave excuses not to wear or even carry the mantle. They understood God's words were weighty and that disobedience could have possibly caused them their lives. PROPHETS SHOULD NOT TAKE THIS CALL LIGHTLY!

RESTORING PROPHETIC INTEGRITY

Waging War in the Heavenlies – Part of the mantle of a Prophet is to war in the heavenlies. Every Prophet will engage in warfare, regardless of whether they want to or not. Without war, they'd be no breakthrough. Ephesians 6:12 states, *"For we do not wrestle against flesh and blood, but against principalities, against powers, against the rulers of the darkness of this age against spiritual hosts of wickedness in the heavenly places."* Prophets' war in the spirit and the results are manifested in the natural.

For example, when the Apostle Paul was in Ephesus, he released the prophetic dimension and the Goddess Diana's structures fell. Acts 19:35 states, "And when the city clerk had quieted the crowd, he said: "Men of Ephesus, what man is there who does not know that the city of the Ephesians is temple guardian of the great goddess Diana, and of the image which fell down from Zeus?" This is an example of the type of warfare Prophets engage in so the word of God can penetrate the territory they are sent to bring the transforming power of God over.

RESTORING PROPHETIC INTEGRITY

A Prophet's Mantle is Confrontational – Prophets' confront battle and wrestle with the kingdom of darkness because of the nature of who they are and the divine mandate of being the mouthpiece of God. Elijah and the Mt Carmel showdown in 1 Kings 18:20-40 is an example of confrontation.

Bring divine alignment to any situation – Prophets have a grace to bring alignment to one's life by speaking and declaring every crooked path be made straight. Isaiah 42:16 states, "I will bring the blind by a way they did not know; I will lead them in paths they have not known. I will make darkness light before them, and crooked places straight. These things I will do for them, and not forsake them."

Another key verse – Isaiah 45:2 – is also important because it paints a visual picture of what takes place when the Prophet starts to prophesy over the lives of God's people. Isaiah 45:2 states, "I will go before you, And make the crooked places straight; I will break in pieces the gates of bronze And cut the bars of iron."

RESTORING PROPHETIC INTEGRITY

This verse speaks to every situation that comes to bind you and hinder what God wants to do in you.

Impart and activate others into the prophetic dimension – Another facet of the Prophet's mantle is to impart the prophetic anointing, activate it and stir it in others. Prophets have a divine grace by God to go forth as His representative and His mouthpiece, and release the prophetic dimension. At times, when impartation and activation is released, there is a quickening in the spirit that causes individuals to immediately start to prophesy.

Intercedes – This facet of the Prophets' mantle intercedes constantly for everything! The Prophet-Intercessor stands in the gap for what appears to be small tasks to great tasks. This is because they are listening to the heartbeat of the Father and praying accordingly. It is under this mantle that God shares his secrets to Prophets for intercessory purposes. Amos 3:7 tells us, "Surely the Lord GOD does nothing, Unless He reveals His secret to His servants the prophets." This is an honorable place to be. There's no greater honor than to have the Father himself share with you specifically what He is doing and getting ready to do.

This is why Moses said he wished all God's people were Prophets. Numbers 11:29 states, *"Then Moses said to him, "Are you zealous for my sake? Oh, that all the LORD's people were prophets and that the LORD would put His Spirit upon them!"* Moses understood that there was a special grace on Prophets so much that he wanted everyone to be able to release the Word of the Lord.

Get instructions through dreams and visions – God gives messages to Prophets through dreams and visions.

Numbers 12:6 tells us, *"Hear now My words: If there is a prophet among you, I, the LORD, make Myself known to him in a vision; I speak to him in a dream."* It is vital that Prophets and prophetic ministers document and write down their dreams because the Lord will speak messages through them. Daniel 7:1

RESTORING PROPHETIC INTEGRITY

says, "In the first year of Belshazzar king of Babylon, Daniel had a dream and visions of his head while on his bed. Then he wrote down the dream, telling the main facts."

Oftentimes, God will show you dreams and visions in pieces, like a puzzle. He may instruct you to write them down because he will give you other pieces later. Then, as you CONTINUE to fast and pray, He will reveal the remainder of the dream to you. Proverbs 25:2 states, "It is the Glory of God to conceal a matter, But the glory of Kings to search it out." It is important that you seek God to get the correct interpretation and understanding of the dream prior to sharing a prophetic interpretation.

Make Declarations and Decrees – Because of the delegated authority and grace Prophets have in the spiritual and in the natural realm. Prophets can make declarations and decrees and create certain results. As Prophets make declarations and decrees, every word that comes out of their mouth establishes something. In 1 Kings 18, Elijah prophesied there would be no rain and there was no rain. Remember – your words have creative power; you should ALWAYS watch what you say!

Whether you are making positive or negative declarations, they will create and establish what you have formed with your mouth. Charles Capp wrote a book called, *"The Tongue – A Creative Force."* In the book, he talks about the power of the words we speak. Prophets move in creative dimensions in the spirit. They establish God's will in the earth. KEEP IN MIND a Prophet is the mouthpiece of God and is specifically assigned to create and release what He is saying.

Prophets prophesy out of their Mantles – a Prophet operating under a Prophets' mantle not only gives personal prophecy, but may also release corporate words over cities, churches, and nations that brings transformation.

When Prophets prophesy out of their mantles, there is a thrust or force in the spirit that causes movement in the atmosphere and situations they are prophesying into. This causes the individual, church, city or nation receiving the word to shift into alignment to the will of God.

Governmental Legislation – another facet of the Prophet's mantle is to legislate and direct what is transpiring in the spirit. This means a Prophet has the ability to shut things down and to cause things to happen. An example of this is the Elijah and the Mt. Carmel showdown in 1 Kings 18:18-40.

Elijah was legislating in the heavenlies by challenging the false governmental structures of Baal and Asherah to call the nation of Israel back to God. This is the strength of the prophetic mantle and the power of prophetic decrees.

Navigating in the Spirit – Prophets know how to navigate in the spirit and chart the course for a divine prophetic atmosphere. They know how to bring a chaotic atmosphere into alignment with the Spirit of God. They are sensitive to the moving of the spirit and know how to sense what direction the Lord is moving.

Prophets release a sound and shout in the heavenlies that drives back the enemy over nations, states, regions and cities. Romans 10:18 tells us, "Their sound has gone out to all the earth, and their words to the ends of the world." (NKJV)

Prophets are Deliverers – Prophets have the ability to be used of the Lord to deliver individuals out of their places of stagnation, complacency and idleness. Prophets have a breaker anointing and they move forth in such power, it causes yokes to be destroyed off of God's people. Hosea 12:13 says it best, "By a prophet the Lord brought Israel out of Egypt, And by a prophet he was preserved." (NKJV)

Prophets are Demonstrative – Throughout a Prophet's ministry, they will constantly demonstrate God message to His people. They just don't prophesy the Word of the Lord; they become the Word of the Lord. Isaiah, Ezekiel and Hosea each demonstrated the Word of the Lord; they became and lived out the Word.

RESTORING PROPHETIC INTEGRITY

Diverse Prophets and Their Purpose

Diverse Types of Prophets

The Bible says the voice of the Lord is as many waters (Revelation 14:2). Just as there are different types of prophetic administrations, so is there diversity in the type of Prophets God has raised up. Today, God is rising up Prophets who are called to the nations. A Prophet to the nations will have an assignment from God to speak into one of the systems of that country, which will release God's glory into that area, to be witnessed by all.

Apostolic Prophets – Apostolic Prophets are Prophets who have an apostolic dimension to their prophetic mantle. These Prophets prophetically see and hear what God is saying and doing, but have a grace to build apostolically according to a prophetic blueprint that the Lord has shown to them.

Issachar Prophets – These Prophets are sons of Issachar that are assigned to discern, understand and declare the times and seasons God has pronounced for each arena.

Prophets to the Local Church – All Prophets are called by God, but they may not be called to the nations. There are some who are called to the local church or church organizations. This is their *metron* (their sphere of influence) which is contained within these boundaries. Many of them would be considered watchmen-type Prophets, like intercessors who watch over, guard, and protect the local church (see Shamar prophetic types). Church Prophets hear from God specifically in regards to the direction, the needs and will of God for the church or organization they are assigned to.

Prophets to Nations – These Prophets go through more intense training than the Prophets to the local church. This additional training equips them to handle each national assignment. Their spiritual jurisdiction covers a global sphere of influence.

Watchmen Prophets – Watchmen Prophets are those who God has called to set watch in the body of

RESTORING PROPHETIC INTEGRITY

Christ. These Prophets will see what the Lord is doing and sound the alarm. Watchmen Prophets will also see the traps and snares of the enemy and warn the people accordingly. They also have the ability to war, stop the enemy at the gate and stop the plans of the enemy from prevailing.

Prophets to the Educational Systems – God has given these Prophets spiritual insight to cause significant breakthroughs in education and teaching strategies. These breakthrough strategies will cause transformational curves in learning for education in the 21st century and beyond.

Prophets to Media and Communication – There are Prophets who declare the word of the Lord in media outlets utilizing new technologies to communicate God's word. These Prophets also receive wisdom downloads for the transformation and expansion of media and communications for our day.

Prophets to Arts and Entertainment – These are Prophets who use the outlets of film, television and music production to develop new venues that will communicate God's ways to society.

Prophets to Government and Politics – These are the Daniels of our day who will go forth in government and politics and that will legislate God's laws into the earth.

Prophets to Religion – These Prophets are specifically called to speak to the religious structures in the earth. They bring reformation to the way God is presented, and release in the earth the strategies that will advance His kingdom.

Prophets to Business and Economics – God gives these modern-day Josephs divine wisdom and corporate strategies to cause breakthroughs in business growth and expansion.

Prophets to Family – These Prophets are both patriarchs and matriarchs who will proclaim the generational blessings on people groups that break generational curses and release the blessing of serving the Lord from generation to generation. Psalm 22:30-31.

REFLECTIVE QUESTIONS

1. In your own words describe a mantle (such as a prophetic mantle).

2. Identify at least five of the functions of a Mantled Prophet that you operate in today.

3. Considering the different types of Prophets, which one describes how you function?

4. Name the most common mandated themes prevalent through all of the Old Testament Prophets?

5. List three Major Prophets and their purposes.

6. List three Minor Prophets and their purposes.

7. List three New Testament Prophets and their purposes.

8. Can Prophets prophesy outside of their mantle? Explain in detail.

REFLECTIVE QUESTIONS

9. What are the roles of the Watchmen Prophets?

10. Define *metron*.

Section 5

Final Thoughts

Final Thoughts

Restoring Prophetic Integrity was penned to help you develop your prophetic gift and ministry. Remember the Holy Spirit will lead and guide you into all truth. Always seek Him for wisdom and understanding; He will pour it out upon you generously.

Your creditability as a Prophet or prophetic minister will be based upon the character you display daily. The Character and Wisdom Keys (Section 3) will be instrumental in helping you maintain your prophetic integrity. And it is vitally important you study the word of God regularly.

Restoring Prophetic Integrity is not intended to override your personal responsibility in the development of your prophetic gift and call. Instead, it is to encourage you to continue to seek the Lord for further revelation.

Scheherazade Daniels —
Prophet
Harvest International Embassy

BIOGRAPHY

SCHEHERAZADE DANIELS

Scheherazade Daniels is a dynamic woman who is also an author, business woman, spiritual coach, college professor, and a Prophet of God.

She walks in a strong mantle for releasing the prophetic dimension in individuals, churches and regions. She carries an anointing for breakthrough in the areas of finance and marketplace strategies.

Scheherazade travels and minsters the principles of the Kingdom at churches, conferences, workshops, seminars, and trainings. She releases her voice through preaching, teaching, praying and prophesying the Word of the Lord. She conducts workshops on the Prophetic, Prayer, Intercession and Spiritual Warfare.

Scheherazade holds a Master's degree in Business Administration and serves as President and CEO of CS Daniels & Associates, LLC. She and her husband, Apostle Clyde, serve as Pastors of Harvest International Embassy, Columbus, Ohio. They reside in Pataskala, Ohio with their three wonderful daughters, and their grandson.

Contact Information

Use any of these methods to contact or connect with Scheherazade:

Scheherazade Daniels

@ScheherazadeD1

Instagram: 007SD

prophetess@harvestintlembassy.org